Trace Elements in Health and Diseases

Dr. Amit Krishna De
Ph.D, F.I.C.N., F.A.E.B., F.N.E.S.A.

Books For All
[A Division of D.K. Publishers Distributors (P) Ltd.]
Delhi - 110 052

Sales Office:
D.K. Publishers Distributors (P) Ltd.
1, Ansari Road, Darya Ganj,
New Delhi - 110002.
Phone : 3261465, 3278368
Fax : 091-011-3264368

ISBN 81-7386-136-6

Published by:
Books For All
[A Division of D.K. Publishers Distributors (P) Ltd.]
Regd.Office : A-6, Nimri Community Centre,
Near Ashok Vihar, Phase - IV,
Delhi - 110052
Phone: 7430113, 7143353
Fax : 091-011-7138265

Laser Type Set at:
FACT COMPUTERS
Delhi-110085.

Printed at:
D.K. Fine Art Press (P) Ltd., Delhi - 110052.

PRINTED IN INDIA

Dedicated
To
My Grand Parents
Mr. Rishi Ram Mitra and
Mrs. Anima Mitra who have always
been a source of Inspiration

FOREWORD

Popular conception lead people to take nutrients for well-being through food. They, even of ancient times, could know by personal experience the linkage of good food to performance. Hence, meat, milk and other good foods, which have been known to be of excellent nutritive value, were sought after. Later, during contemporary period there had been specific craze for proteins from food and then vitamins. This desire has now been enlarged for metals so much that people tend to take tablets of vitamins and minerals, with or without medical prescription.

Some metals like calcium, phosphorus and iron are necessary in larger amounts, as a RDA (recommended daily dietary allowance) chart will show and some in around trace concentrations. The latter group is very interesting: essential but in low concentrations and toxic in more than desirable or tolerable concentrations. The excess amounts generally cannot be flushed out in many cases by the kidneys even if the salts are water soluble unlike the water soluble vitamins. These accumulate like the fat soluble vitamins and are similarly toxic. It is as if the excess having no remaining work to perform interferes with the work of others specially of metals of similar properties and hence of the same valency.

Essentiality of many of the metals was not apparent effortlessly. Small amounts of the requirements could be met easily through food even without being aware of the facts. Vegetation extracts metals from soils and to some extent from water. This absorption can be generalized, and also specific as some plants may have a special faculty of concentrating some metals. Water hyacinth had been lauded for concentrating some metal pollutants of water. Tradesmen in order to gain larger allowances for lead would argue, though unfoundedly, that turmeric concentrates more lead from the. soil than other vegetation. Iodine of the soil ingested primarily through vegetables has been adequate to prevent goitre but not in terrain region where rain washing denuded the soil of iodine. But now this endemic deficiency has become generalized because soil got poorer in iodine in a generalized manner. Zinc deficiency heard of in the middle east was not prevalent in India, but is possibly so now. These scares and some previous knowledge of trace nutrition (e.g., copper for haemoglobin and fluorine against dental caries) attracted attention for metal supplementation.

Regarding toxicity of these metals, iron, copper, lead, cadmium, mercury, chromium, arsenic, nickel, cobalt, aluminium, tin etc., have been recognised as pollutants of food and water in amounts exceeding the permitted concentration.

Metal metabolism and toxicity is a very active field of research in bio-inorganic chemistry. Newer observations are coming to light. While deficiency has been ascribed to poor intake, and toxicity to excess, there can be variants; preliminary results indicate that there is induced by low dose radiation zinc deficiency which is known to decimate sexual development to some extent. While working on arsenic toxicity from tubewell water, it was discovered that better nutrition as of rich men can ward off the toxicity. Hence, here is a suggestion that protective food can immunise a metal intoxication of arsenic. Aluminium hitherto believed non toxic has now been found to be toxic to the extent of engendering Alzheimer's disease.

The above-mentioned words, introductory of the present monograph, may indicate that subject of metal metabolism is still not known fully, is an active field of research and of much popular concern. I am sure the author, a capable scientist and an expert in this line, has set his work in the perspective of nutrition and toxicity of metals, and hence of physical and mental well-being.

Dr. B. R. Roy, Ph.D.
Former Director of Central Food Laboratory and
Central Forensic Science Laboratory and
Visiting Professor of Jadavpur University

CONTENTS

INTRODUCTION

The science of human nutrition is mainly concerned with defining the optimum amounts of the constituents of food necessary to achieve or maintain health throughout the full span of life in all groups of the population. Thus, the pregnant woman, the newborn, the growing child, the adult and the old person—all have specific dietary requirements for their different physiological states. A faulty diet in which the amounts of nutrients are inadequate or in the wrong proportions lead eventually to disease or may contribute to the development of disease. Nutrition therefore plays a part in both preventive and curative medicine, and the effectiveness of its role depends upon continued investigations into the metabolism of nutrients.

Development in knowledge has indicated that the idea of nutrition may not be restricted to protein, carbohydrate, lipid and vitamins but also to minerals, particularly to those required in trace amounts. Trace elements may be categorised as follows (i) those for which humans have a well defined need, such as iron, iodine and zinc, (ii) those for which estimated, safe and adequate daily dietary intakes have been established such as copper, manganese, fluoride, chromium, selenium and molybdenum, (iii) those that are important to certain animals but for which human requirements have not been well defined such as nickel, silicon and (iv) those that have some toxic effects on the body such as aluminium, arsenic, and yet show well defined functions.

These essential and important trace elements are required in very small amounts, in the range of micrograms to milligrams. The determination of optimal dietary requirements to avoid even marginal deficiencies is a challenge to nutrition researchers. The nutrient analysis of a trace element cannot be the sole index of its contribution to the diet. The chemical form in which a trace element is consumed is very important. The importance of trace elements has been recognized in animal nutrition for several years. In contrast, their place in human nutrition was established only recently. One of the first studies demonstrating the need for trace elements in human nutrition was in 1961 when growth retardation, hypogonadism and anemia in zinc deficient individuals living in the Middle East was reported. Subsequently, other syndromes of trace element deficiency, particularly due to congenital abnormalities have become evident in the ensuing years. Among these are acrodermatitis enteropathica caused by zinc deficiency, Menke'skinkyhair syndrome due to copper deficiency, and cardiomyopathy due to selenium deficiency.

At present the trace elements recognised as essential for man are zinc, copper, chromium, selenium, iron, iodine, cobalt (as vitamin B_{12}) and possibly manganese. Whiie fluoride is important for caries resistance to the enamel of teeth there are no other known indications for this element. Other trace elements such as molybdenum, nickel, aluminium, silicone, tin, vanadium and arsenic, while essential in animals are not yet been proved to be essential for man and at present, there is insufficient information to recommend use of these elements during total parenteral nutrition therapy.

Most of the elements though beneficial in trace amounts may show a variety of toxic side effects if administered in high doses. Arsenic, in particularly, has been reported repeatedly in the past to exhibit different toxic effects that have eventually lead to death. Recently, Aluminium has been found to cause Alzhemer's disease, which is a major headache of the twenty first century. With increasing environmental pollution, metal toxicity is slowly becoming a great concern for the scientists, and it is time that people should start thinking anew.

I am grateful to 'Books For All' a Division of D.K Publishers Distributors (P) Ltd. for publishing a book exclusively written on trace elements. This is probably the first of it's kind in the area of nutrition. I am also indebted to Dr. B.R. Roy, Ex-Director, Central Food Laboratory and Ex-Director, Central Forensic Science Laboratory, Calcutta, for writing the foreword of this book. I am also grateful to my parents whose constant encouragement and co-operation have provided me with the strength of undergoing such a vital task. I also acknowledge the assistance of my wife,

Mrs. Minakshi De, B.Ed, M.Sc., in preparing this manuscript. I dedicate this book to my grand parents who have been a constant source of inspiration to my work.

Amit Krishna De

1

IODINE

Iodine is an essential trace element required for human growth and development. The daily requirement of iodine may range from 3 μg/kg body wt/day. Recently based on the urinary excretion of iodine and balance studies, iodine requirements have been estimated to be between a minimum of 50 μg to a maximum of 100 μg. A generally accepted desirable intake of iodine in adults is 150-200 μg/day. The WHO recommendations on the daily intake of iodine for different age groups are given in Table 1.

Table-1
Who Recommendations

Age	Recommended intake (μg)
0-12 months	40 - 50
1-10 years	70 - 120
11 years - adulthood	120 - 150
Pregnancy and lactation	175 - 200

SOURCES OF IODINE

Iodine is concentrated (as iodides) in the top soil of the earth and absorbed by food crops. About 90 per cent of daily needs of human is met from food and 10 per cent from water. Some species of seaweed are the richest sources of iodine in nature. Consequently, sea fish that feed on such seaweed form an excellent source in iodine. Actually the concentration of iodine in sea water is low but sea life such as algae, fish, oysters concentrate iodine and are good source of iodine. Plant foods also provide iodine but the amount depends on the soil content. In regions subject to frequent floodings, the soil may be stripped of its iodine and the food crops, vegetables and fruits grown in that region are deficient in iodine.

The iodine content of drinking water (as iodines) in goitrous area is 3-16 μg/litre as compared to 5-64 μg/litre in non-goitrous areas. The values for bovine milk ranges from 11-13 μg/100 g. The iodine content of fish range between 28 and 55 μg/100 g. Only certain types of fish which are occasionally seen in the sea-coast (cod/heddock) contain more iodine (175 μg/100 g) than fresh water fish. The iodine content of egg is about 50 μg/100 g and is concentrated more in the white portion. The iodine content of some common Indian foods are given in Table 2.

Table - 2
Iodine Content of Some Common Indian Foods (µg/100 g)

Foods	Region	
	Goitrous	Non-Goitrous
CEREALS AND MILLETS		
Rice	10	40
Wheat	15	32
Maize	11	33
Bajra	26	42
Sorghum	21	73
PULSES		
Soyabean	4	49
Bengalgram	13	33
Blackgram	17	48
Redgram	19	28
Horsegram	17	26
Lentil	4	13
Cowpea	22	39
OILSEEDS		
Mustard	—	55
Groundnut	14	47
Sesame	29	43

(Contd.)

Foods	Region	
	Goitrous	Non-Goitrous
VEGETABLES		
Amaranth leaves	8	15
Cucumber	5	11
Curry leaves	—	16
Spinach	—	4
Mint leaves	—	9
Tomato	—	2
Ladies finger	—	5
Cabbage	—	3
Carrot	—	6
Brinjal	—	2
Cauliflower	—	1
Snakegourd	—	3
FRUITS		
Apple	—	5
Orange	—	11
Banana	—	16
Custard Apple	—	3
Grapes	—	11
Papaya	—	12

Table - 3
Recommended Daily Dietary Allowances for Iodine

	Age (Years)	Weight (kg)	Weight (lb)	Height (cm)	Height (in)	Iodine (μg)
Infants	0.0 - 0.5	6	13	60	24	40
	0.5 - 1.0	9	20	71	28	50
Children	1 - 3	13	29	90	35	70
	4 - 6	20	44	112	44	90
	7 - 10	28	62	132	52	120
Males	11 - 14	45	99	157	62	150
	15 - 18	66	145	176	69	150
	19 - 22	70	154	177	70	150
	23 - 50	70	154	178	70	150
	51+	70	154	178	70	150
Females	11 - 14	46	101	157	62	150
	15 - 18	55	120	163	64	150
	19 - 22	55	120	163	64	150
	23 - 50	55	120	163	64	150
	51+	55	120	163	64	150
Pregnant						+25
Lactating						+50

SOURCE: Food and Nutrition Board, *Recommended Dietary Allowances*, 9th ed. (Washington, D.C.: The National Academy of Sciences, 1980).

ABSORPTION AND METABOLISM

Iodine present as iodine in foods is readily absorbed from the gastrointestinal tract. Other forms of iodine in foods are reduced to iodide before absorption. Iodine is rapidly distributed in the body through circulation. Probably all cells of the body contains iodine. The concentration of iodine in thyroid gland is around 70-80 per cent of the total iodine content of the body. Most of the iodine is taken up by the thyroid gland for synthesis of the hormone and the rest is excreted by Kidney. The iodine content in blood of normal man varies from 3-20 μg per 100 ml serum and is of diagnostic importance in thyroid diseases. Plasma carries about 5-8 μg iodine bound to plasma proteins known as protein bound iodine or PBI. Because iodine intake in excess of requirement is excreted primarily through the urine, urinary iodine is a good measure of iodine status.

The mechanism of iodine metabolism involves the following steps:

(1) the uptake of blood iodide by thyroid
(2) storage of this iodide as inorganic iodide
(3) enzymatic oxidation of iodide to iodine
(4) iodination of protein bound tyrosine to monoiodotyrosine/diiodotyrosine to form thyroxine
(5) release of thyroid hormones into blood
(6) association of thyroxine with blood proteins
(7) distribution to tissues and metabolism *via* deiodination
(8) excretion through the kidney.

DEFICIENCY

Iodine deficiency in diet occurs in goitrerous regions where the soil contains very little iodide and the fruits and vegetables grown in these area are deficient in iodine.

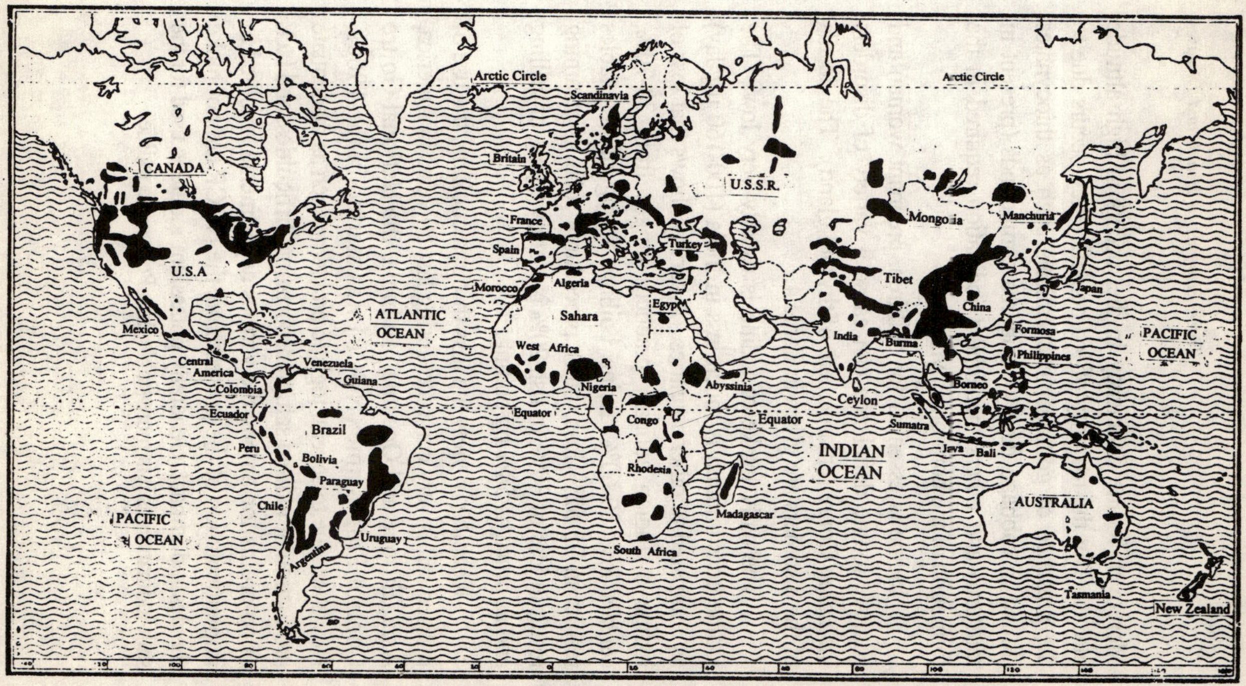

FIGURE – 1 Goiter areas of the world. (Chilean Iodine Educational Bureau, London)

Moreover, iodine deficiency in diet occurs in high altitude places. But the majority of iodine deficiency occurs due to the presence of goitrogenic chemicals such as thiocynates (found in cabbage family), thiourea compounds (present in mustard) and others that inhibit iodination required in the formation of the hormone thyroxine.

Iodine is essential for children, pregnant woman and adults. Iodine deficiency can cause a variety of disorders including Goitre (enlargement of thyroid gland). The details of the disorders are given in Table 4.

The daily intake of iodine is usually very low. The iodine consumption is much less in India (100-160 μg/day) as compared to other countries. A survey shows that loss of iodine in Indian culinary practices ranges from 20-70%, cereals lose 30-60% during boiling, frying of vegetables results in 25-52% loss, other procedures such as steaming result in loss of 30%, in fish 20% is lost by frying of grilling and as much as 58% by boiling.

Keeping in view the loss through cooking, the use of iodised salt is very common during last 50 years in America, Asia, Europe and Oceania. In India, the National Goitre Control Programme (NGCP) was started in the 1960s. However, due to several logistic problems such as inadequate production of iodised salt, transportation difficulties, and lack of co-ordination among the various departments involved in implementation of the programme, the NGCP did not make the desired impact. Generally potassium iodate is used for the sallt iodination as it is more stable than Potassium iodide.

Table - 4
Effects of Iodine Deficiency Disorders

CHILDREN
* Lowered IQ (10 to 15 points)
* Impaired school performance
* Mental retardation
* Delayed motor development
* Growth failure or stunting
* Muscular disorders
* Speech defects
* Hearing defects
PREGNANT WOMAN
* Abortions
* Stillbirths
* Infant deaths
* Impaired brain development of the foetus
* Birth of iodine deficient babies - cretins
ADULTS
* Lack of energy
* Goitre with its complications - thyroid deficiency, impaired mental function
* Reduced productivity

EXCESS INTAKE OF IODINE

Iodine intake upto 1000 μg/day showed no adverse physiologic reactions as was evident by a study conducted by American Medical Association. Though normal people exposed to excess iodine remain euthyroid through adaptive mechanisms, adverse effects may be seen in susceptible individuals and in patients with pre-existing abnormalities of the thyroid gland. It might contribute to the development of Hashimoto thyroiditis iodide and colloid goitre and thyroid carcinoma in such cases. However there is little indication that iodine in the amounts consumed through prophylaxis programme influences the development of any of these thyroid diseases.

IODINE SUPPLEMENTATION

In some localities iodide has been added to the water supply, but this method is not widely used, partly because it does not benefit rural areas, partly because consumption of water by different individuals varies greatly and partly because it is not economical. Milk and eggs have been iodized by incorporating some form of iodine in the diets of cows and hens but this is not done on a large scale. In two goitrous areas of Australia, iodates have been included in bread as a routine procedure. However, a survey showed that the weekly consumption of iodine from iodated bread was much lower than that secured from a tablet containing potassium iodide.

As indicated earlier, salt is generally considered the most acceptable carrier for iodine. At present the level of salt iodization permitted in the United States is 0.1 to 1 part in 10,000. Thus if 10 grams (about 2 teaspoons) of salt are consumed per day, a person would receive from 0.5 to 1 mg iodine, an amount in excess of that needed but not enough to be harmful. Because the iodide may volatilize, a stabilizer such as sodium carbonate sometimes is added. If this is not done the salt offered for sale should be analyzed at intervals by the state health department to be sure the content of iodine is upto standard.

The iodate has been found to be better adapted for fortification than the iodide since it is a more stable compound, especially in areas where moisture and high temperatures prevail. It is not used in salt sold for human consumption in the United States, however; the FDA approves potassium iodide and cuprous iodide, both at a level of .01 per cent. Iodates are used as an improver in bread; the amount incorporated is regulated by the FDA. It is thought that these iodine compounds, secured from dairy products and bread, along with iodized salt and natural foods rich in iodine, make the American diet adequate in respect to this mineral.

2

IRON

Eggs are a valuable source of iron, but milk, the most complete single food, is low in iron and the daily diet recommended for the adult supplies only a very small fraction of the need. Since lean meat furnishes considerable iron, it should be eaten daily. Dried beans and the molasses added when they are baked, furnish an inexpensive and good source of iron. Dried fruits are another good source. Of the leafy vegetables, parsley is the highest in iron content but it is a negligible source since it is used chiefly as a garnish. In general, the green vegetables, such as spinach and leaf lettuce are richer sources than are those with little chlorophyll such as cabbage, celery and head lettuce. Roots and tubers generally furnish little iron. However, potatoes, because of their daily consumption, supply a measurable amount. This is specially true when the whole potato is eaten as it may be when baked or boiled in the skin. Baking chocolate and coco are good sources of iron. One tablespoon of cocoa sometimes used in making one serving of the beverage contains almost one mg of iron.

Outer layers of grains contain most of the iron, and thus use of the whole product may be recommended. Flour varies considerably in it's iron contribution, whole wheat flour has 3.3 mg iron per 100 gm. Enriched all-purpose flour 2.9 mg, unenriched all-purpose flour 0.8 mg, cake flour 0.5 mg. Dark, medium and light rye flours contain 4.5, 2.6 and 1.1 mg iron per 100 gm flour respectively. Iron is probably the most difficult of all nutrients to obtain in sufficient amounts in the daily diet. Hence, a planned diet chart should be prepared for iron consumption. (Table -1)

Table - 1
Distribution of Iron in Daily Diet

Food Groups	Iron Content	
	mg/100 gm	percent
Mili Cheese	10.2	2.2
Meat, fish, eggs, legume	182.3	39.6
Darkgreen & deep yellow vegetables	10.3	2.2
Citrus fruits, tomatoes	12.8	2.8
Potatoes	64.5	14.1
Grain products	148.2	32.2

FERRITIN

Ferritin is a water soluble protein with variable iron content found in bone marrow, liver, spleen and intestinal wall. It consists of a protein shell with the micelles of ferric hydroxide-ferric phosphate complex. When treated with reducing agent at acid pH, the iron of ferritin can be removed completely by dialysis, to give apoferritin, a colourless protein (M.Wt 465,000). The bulk of the ferritin iron is in the ferric state but a small portion exists in the ferrous state at or near the surface.

ABSORPTION

The ordinary diet contains 10-20 mg of iron but less than 10 per cent of intake is absorbed. This is because iron present in body can be used over again. Part of the iron of our foodstuffs is converted to iron salts by the gastric HCl and then reduced by the various reducing agents such as glutathione, ascorbic acid and many SH (sulfhydryl) groups of protein amino acids. Iron ingested largely in the ferric form must be reduced to the ferrous state in the stomach and intestine before it can pass through the intestinal mucosa into blood stream. Ferrous ion is absorbed especially in the upper duodenum. As absorption of iron occurs, the concentration of ferritin increases in the same areas of the intestine. The iron in the ferrous form being more soluble than ferric form enters the mucosal cells and is stored in ferritin as ferric hydroxide. When the content of iron in ferritin decreases to some critical point, more iron from the intestine is absorbed into the mucosal cells.

Actually, very little dietary iron is absorbed by the adult and very little is excreted in the urine. Most of the dietary iron is eliminated with the faeces. The absorption of iron from the intestine is controlled in such a way that it's accumulation in the tissues in toxic amounts do not occur normally since there is no other way to excrete excess iron. Once absorbed, the mineral is carried by the plasma. There it is converted into the ferrous state and bound to transferrin. Iron passes quickly into the bone marrow where the red blood cells are formed. The portion not needed for storage and haemoglobin formation is returned to the plasma which carries it to liver/spleen for most of the iron in the body is in the haemoglobin of red blood cells, that functions in carrying oxygen and continuing oxidation reduction reactions within cells. The haemoglobin of the dying red cells is degraded to amino acids, bile pigments and iron. The iron is incorporated into tissue ferritin, as well as liberated into the plasma to continue its cycle. The tissue ferritin serves as source house of iron taking care of excess iron and releasing iron for maintaining a plasma concentration suitable to the needs of bone marrow where it finds its way into haemoglobin of newly born red cell. Catalase and cytochromes are other non-proteins synthesized in addition to haemoglobin. Ferritin is found in the human placenta which suggests that iron is released from maternal plasma to foetal plasma.

Hence factors affecting metabolic cycles of iron include—

(1) the rate of breakdown of haemoglobin

(2) uptake by the bone marrow (for red blood cell synthesis)

(3) removal and storage by tissues

(4) absorption from the GI tract (Gastro intestinal tract)

(5) rate of formation and decomposition of transferrin

(6) concentration of Copper

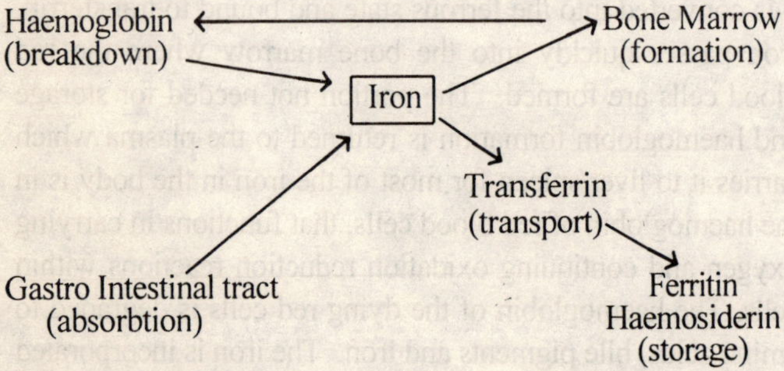

HEMOSIDERIN

It is an insoluble Iron-protein complex found also in liver, spleen and bone marrow. The two forms appear to be functionally indistinguishable and may represent only different physical forms. This is also a protein complexed with Ferric hydroxide and other substances. It has been suggested that hemosiderin may be largely a breakdown product of ferritin.

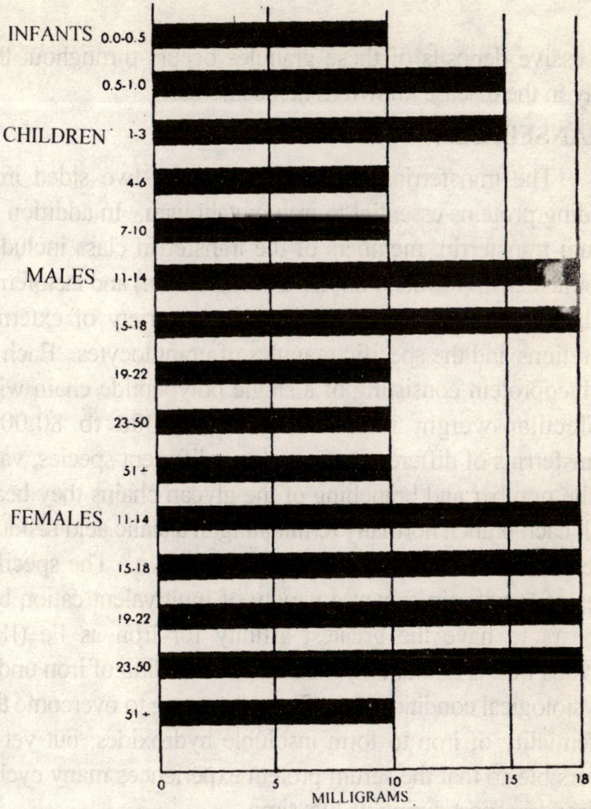

Fig.1. Comparison of recommended daily dietary allowances of iron between various ages, both sexes, and for pregnancy and lactation. The increased requirement during pregnancy cannot be met by the iron content of typical American diets nor by the existing iron stores of many women; therefore the use of 30-60 mg of supplemental iron is recommended. Iron needs during lactation are not substantially different from those of non-pregnant women, but continued supplementation of the mother for 2-3 months after parturition is advisable in order to replenish stores depleted by pregnancy. (Adapted from *Recommended Dietary Allowances*, 9th edition, Food and Nutrition Board, National Research Council – National Academy of Sciences, 1980).

Excessive deposits of these granules occurs throughout the body in the disease known as hemosiderosis.

TRANSFERRIN

The transferrins comprise a class of two sided iron binding proteins essential to iron metabolism. In addition to serum transferrin, members of the transferrin class includes ovotransferrin (formerly known as conalbumin) and lactoferrin or lactotransferrin, identified in milk, a variety of external secretions and the specific granules of granulocytes. Each is a glycoprotein consisting of a single polypeptide chain with molecular weight in the range of 75,000 to 80,000. Transferrins of different types or from different species, vary in the number and branching of the glycan chains they bear, with each branch normally terminating in a sialic acid residue. The function of the sugar chains is unknown. The specific sites of transferrin accept a variety of multivalent cation but appears to have the greatest affinity for iron as Fe (III). Ferrous iron is bound only weakly. The binding of iron under physiological conditions is sufficiently strong to overcome the potentiality of iron to form insoluble hydroxides, but yet is reversible so that the serum protein experiences many cycles of iron transport during its life- time.

Three separate events are often distinguished in the pathway of iron donation by transferrin to haemoglobin-synthesizing reticulocytes: (a) the binding of protein to its specific receptor on the plasma membrane, (b) the release of iron borne by the protein, and (c) the return of iron depleted but otherwise intact protein to the circulation for a new cycle of iron transport.

The iron is transported to tissues and storage depots by transferrin. Once in circulation, the iron molecules are transported throughout the plasma bound tightly to transferrin until they are delivered to a transferrin receptor on the membrane of a target cell. From there the iron is transferred perhaps, *via* another intracellular metalloprotein, to the storage protein, Ferritin. Once complexed to ferritin, the iron molecules are available for incorporation into iron-containing compounds. Alternately, they may be stored as soluble ferritin or insoluble haemosiderin, usually in lysosomes. In normal state, then, iron is never found. More than 70 per cent of the normal body Iron is located in biologically active compounds including haemoglobin, myoglobin, and a wide variety of heme containing enzymes. Small amounts of iron function in non heme containing enzymes as cofactors or are incorporated into a variety of metalloflavoproteins. Of the 30 per cent reserve, most is present in the relatively non reactive storage forms, ferritin and hemosiderin.

DEFICIENCY

Anemias represent the most common derangement of iron metabolism with abnormally low concentration of haemoglobin in the circulation. The anemias may be due to iron deficiency in the diet, known as *nutritional anemia.* This condition occurs when there is insufficient supply of iron to replace the daily loss. This disease is common in the case of infant and young children. This may be due to –

(1) Inadequate intake (low meat).
(2) Inadequate absorption (GI disturbances-diarrhoea, intestinal diseases)
(3) Excessive loss of blood (hemorrhage).

Treatment includes

(a) Addition of ferrous sulphate to diet
(b) iron-dextran injection (for persons with inadequate absorption)

An excess amount of iron may accumulate in the tissues because of the absence of an excretory pathway for iron. This happens in *aplastic* or *haemolytic anemia* where many blood transfusions have been given over a period of years. This is known as *haemosiderosis* which may be accompanied by a bronzed pigmentation of the skin, liver damage with signs of cirrhosis, diabetes and a pancreatic fibrosis—a condition called bronze diabetes.

Polycythemia, an increase in blood haemoglobin above normal levels is associated with an overproduction of erythrocytes despite life span of a red cells remaining normal. High altitudes or an atmosphere low in content may induce polycythemia.

Idiopathic hemochromatosis is due to hyperabsorption of dietary non heme iron. It may also be due to a defect in the ability of the reticuloendothelial cells to retain iron, which results in early saturation of circulating transferrin and in increased loading of parenchymal cells. This is a genetic disorder and may be linked with HLA-A_3, HLA-B_7 and HLA-B_{14} antigens on chromosome 6.

In *pernicious anemia* there is lack of a substance (which produces the body or stroma of the red blood cells) that causes deficiency in cell number and abnormal shape and size. There is involvement of two factors an extrinsic one found in food (vitamin B_{12}) and an intrinsic factor that is stored in the liver. This is treated with folic acid, vitamin B_{12} and liver extract.

Hemorrhagic anemia develops due to internal bleeding which occurs in peptic ulcer. Excessive loss of blood also may occur during the menstrual period or from a wound or accident. This anemia may not be detected for some time, especially when associated with internal bleeding, which may occur with peptic ulcer. Too frequent blood donations may result in this type of anemia. For each pint of blood donated approximately 200 mg of iron are lost from the body. To replace this loss over a period of year the daily intake should be increased by 0.7 mg. Most rapid regeneration occurred when the daily diet contained 90 gm of protein. Oral therapy using simple, soluble ferrous salts, is often advocated in treatment of haemorrhagic anemia. For those who cannot tolerate or absorb oral preparations, parenteral administration may be used. Iron dextran, iron sorbitol and dexiferron are the three best available preparations for parenteral use.

Hypochromic anemia results from a deficiency of iron in the diet. Developing gradually, this disorder is associated with weakness, a feeling of fatigue, poor appetite and pallor.

Symptoms may also include constipation, lusterless, brittle, and flatterened nails, dyspea on exersion and achlorhydia. A blood test shows a low haemoglobin level but the red cell count may be within the normal range, serum iron value and transferrin saturation are decreased and iron binding capacity is increased. Treatment includes administration of iron salts and a diet planned to favour absorption of iron and blood regeneration.

Ferrous iron is recommended for therapeutic use in 3-5 divided doses daily since only a relatively small per cent of any given amount can be absorbed. It should be given when the upper GI tract is free of phosphate which combines with iron to make unabsorbable residue. If given with an infant's meal of milk and cereal, iron is less available. Enteric coated ferrous iron tablets or iron capsules containing delayed release granules are not advised because the absorption of iron is less efficient in the lower part of the small intestine.

Pernicious anemia is not fundamentally a dietary disease. Instead of a shortage of food iron, there is lack of substance which produces the body or storms of the red blood cells, the cells are deficient in number and abnormal in shape and size. Because the haemoglobin is relatively high there is high colour index. There is also a deficient gastric secretion. Actually two factors are involved in the prevention and cure of the anemia, an extrinsic one found in the food and an intrinsic one found normally in gastric secretion but lacking in that of the pernicious anemia patient. The intrinsic factor may be stored in the liver. This theory explains the efficacy of liver, liver extract, and stomach extract in curing the dread disease. Vitamin B_{12} is now known as the extrinsic factor. Folic acid has a favorable effect on the faulty blood condition in pernicious anemia but is not effective in treating the abnormalities in the nervous system. Both folic acid and vitamin B_{12} are prescribed in treatment of pernicious anemia.

THERAPY FOR DISORDERS OF IRON EXCESS

Three forms of iron excess are examined. The first type is acute iron poisoning, for which therapy is designed to bind the sudden excess of iron in the body to render it nontoxic and promote its excretion. The second type is a specific form of chronic iron overload, hereditary hemochromatosis, a disorder due to the slow accumulation of excessive body iron loads that can be completely removed with reversal of many aspects of the disease. The third type is the chronic iron overload resulting from multiple blood transfusions for chronic anemia such as beta-thalassemia. Treatment of the third type of iron excess involves partial iron removal and only partial benefits. Each of these disorders poses different problems and requires a different strategy for successful therapy.

(a) Acute Iron Poisoning

Reports of toxicity after the oral ingestion of iron medications go back more than a hundred years, when doctors began prescribing various iron-containing mixtures for the alleviation of anemia and chlorosis. Iron toxicity was relatively rare then because of the poor absorbability of the iron in medication such as Blaud's pills (a mixture of ferrous sulphate and potassium carbonate that promptly formed insoluble ferric carbonate in the gastrointestinal tract). The first real appreciation of the dangers of acute iron intoxication was the report in 1947, in which it was described the deaths of two children after the ingestion of a proprietary mixture containing the sulphates of iron, manganese, and copper. Forbes showed conclusively that iron sulphate was the offending agent. Since that time ferrous sulphate has been implicated in many additional cases of acute iron toxicity and many fatalities. However, ferrous sulphate is not unique in causing toxicity. Almost all forms of iron that are soluble and absorbed by the gastrointestinal tract have been implicated in toxicity.

Since the report, the dangers of accidental iron poisoning have been stressed in numerous case reports and reviews. Iron poisoning in a problem confined almost entirely to children, usually between 1 and 5 years of age young enough to be curious but not old enough to be careful. In adults, iron poisoning is almost invariably a consequence of suicide attempts. Typically, the toddler finds a bottle of brightly coloured, sugar-coated iron tablets carelessly left within his reach. If he manages to eat a large number of them before he is discovered, he is likely to add to the statistics of the local poison control center. In recent years, iron poisoning has ranked in the top five causes of poisoning in children under 5 which may vary considerably. Death may occur from ingestion of as little as 2 to 4 gm ferrous sulphate (6-12 tablets). Iron toxicity with complete recovery may occur after doses as large as 14 gm (70 tablets). The uncertainty of the number of tablets ingested in most cases of childhood iron poisoning requires a cautious approach in management of this potentially serious condition.

The clinical course of iron poisoning is usually divided into four phases. The first phase, which often appears within an hour after iron ingestion, includes vomiting with abdominal pain, sometimes there is hematemesis, diarrhoea, and melena. Pallor, lassitude, and peripheral vascular collapse may supervene with hyperventilation from profound metabolic acidosis. If supportive therapy is not given promptly, coma and death may occur within 4 to 6 hr. The second phase is a period of clinical improvement and the reversal of all previous symptoms after vigorous treatment. Improvement may be sustained and proceed to complete recovery or it may be deceptive. The third phase may begin within 12 to 48 hr after ingestion of the iron pills. The patient often manifests progressive deterioration with fever, jaundice, convulsions, coma, and death. The fourth phase, which occurs in some survivors, is the late appearance of pyloric stenosis or gastric fibrosis with obstructive symptoms in about 6 weeks.

The pathogenesis of these clinical symptoms include erosion and hemorrhagic necrosis of the mucosa of the gastrointestinal tract that is a direct consequence of high local iron concentrations. High concentrations of iron absorbed into the plasma exceed the transferrin binding capacity and circulate loosely bound to albumin and other plasma proteins. This iron is readily taken up by many cells, and metabolic acidosis is probably due to diffuse mitochondrial damage and profound impairment of cellular metabolism, especially the enzyme involved in the citric acid cycle. Hepatic cell swelling and necrosis lead to the jaundice, while similar swelling of cells in the heart, kidneys, and brain is evidence of their damage, responsible for circulatory failure, renal shutdown, convulsions, and coma. Disseminated intravascular coagulation may also be observed.

Treatment can be divided conveniently into three components and must be initiated promptly and vigorously. Even if there is doubt about a significant ingestion of iron, treatment is imperative. The first approach to treatment is to remove any unabsorbed iron from the stomach by inducing vomiting with syrup of ipecac and lavage of the stomach with a large bore tube to recover any remaining tablets. The stomach is irrigated with sodium bicarbonate solution to precipitate the iron and make it less absorbable. The second component of treatment is the general supportive measures of treating shock with appropriate electrolyte solutions, vasopressors, and blood transfusions, correction of the acidosis, and the administration of oxygen. The third component of treatment is specific therapy to reduce the hyperferremia with the chelating agent deferoxamine. Deferoxamine may be given orally to bind iron that remains in the gastrointestinal tract after induced vomiting and lavage and prevent it from contributing further to the toxic plasma iron levels.

For most patients who are not in shock, deferoxamine is given intramuscularly. For patients in shock, the deferoxamine must be given intravenously, since intramuscular doses might not be mobilized adequately. The intravenous dose rate should not exceed 15 mg/kg body weight/hr, faster rates are associated with hypotension. One measure of the efficacy of deferoxamine-induced urinary iron removal can be assessed by the depth of the red colour of the ferrioxamine in the urine.

Table - 2

Treatment of Acute Iron Poisoning

Treatment of Acute Iron Poisoning
Remove iron from the gastrointestinal tract
Induce vomiting with ipecac
lavage stomach with $NaHCO_3$ solution
Abdominal X-rays for iron tablets
General supportive measures
Treat shock
Correct acidosis
Administer oxygen
Chelate iron with deferoxamine

(b) Hereditary Hemochromatosis

In contrast to the dramatic acute iron intoxication in a small child, hereditary hemochromatosis presents the pattern of a subtle chronic build-up of iron overload that may not be recognized for 50 years or more.

Recent identification of certain HLA antigens (A_3, B_7, B_{14}) that are closely linked to a hemochromatosis gene on human chromosome 6 has been carried out. With the HLA markers the genetic inheritance of hemochromatosis has been clarified as an autosomal recessive disorder. Pedigree studies of a patient's family by HLA follow the identification of homozygotes with actual or potential full-blown disease and heterozygotes with only a mild derangement of iron metabolism and limited increase of iron stores below the threshold for tissue damage. The most sensitive screening test for iron overload is an elevated serum transferrin saturation. Confirming evidence includes an elevated serum ferritin concentration and, ultimately, increased amounts of iron determined chemically and histologically on a needle biopsy sample of the liver.

The pathogenesis of hemochromatosis involves some still-undefined abnormality that permits increased iron absorption from a normal diet. The small increment of iron absorbed, in the range of 3 or 4 mg/day in excess of requirements to maintain iron balance, is carried by the plasma transferrin to storage depots, primarily the parenchymal cells of the liver. Gradual build-up for many years may go unrecognized, but eventually the iron pills over into other tissues, specially various endocrine glands. Iron deposited as ferritin and hemosiderin within hepatocytes appears to be a low grade stimulus to fibrosis by mechanisms that remains obscure since they have been quite resistant to production in experimental animals. Iron leads to other forms of cellular dysfunction, possibly by free radical generation, lysosomal damage and lipid peroxidation. Regardless of the mechanism, the eventual results are organ dysfunction and the most seriously affected organs are the liver, the heart, pancreas and other endocrine glands as well as the synovlum of various joints. In the liver, there is a close corelation between iron concentration and fibrosis. Cirrhosis usually occurs when the iron concentration is greater than 3 per cent of dry weight.

The close association between the amount of excess tissue iron, organ dysfunction, and symptoms of disease led to the idea of removing the iron to try to improve the patient's clinical condition. In 1949, geriodic phlebotomies for iron removal from patients with hereditary hemochromatosis was introduced. This procedure has been the principal treatment ever since. The rational for phlebotomy is disarmingly simple. For each pint of blood removed from the patient, about 200 mg iron will be removed in the haemoglobin of the erythrocytes. This haemoglobin deficit in the blood is made up by the withdrawal of iron from the excessive ferritin and hemosiderin storage depots. As long as erythropoiesis remains unimpaired, iron is transferred from the tissues to the blood and is removed by phlebotomy until the expanded body iron stores are reduced to normal levels. In practice, the removal of a pint of blood each week is well tolerated by most patients, and the excessive iron stores of 20 gm or more are reduced to normal in 1 to 3 years. More rapid rates of iron removal, with phlebotomies twice a week, or three times weekly, can be eliminated, examination of liver biopsies reveal that the hepatocytes are freed of their iron burden. This ability to remove iron completely and to maintain the normal iron status indefinitely by sporadic phlebotamies permits an assessment of the improvement of organ function after iron removal.

3

COPPER

The daily need of copper is around 2 mg. Copper is widely distributed in food and a dietary deficiency is not likely to occur in human beings except in infants fed on milk diet exclusively. The copper content in certain food stuffs are (per 100 gm):

Liver - 44.1 mg	Fish - 1.7 mg
Nuts - 11.6 mg	Cow milk - 0.9-1.7 mg
Cereals - 4.7 mg	Leafy vegetables -1.2mg

The richest sources of copper in floods, are shellfish, especially cysters and canned crab; liver, particularly calf's liver; nuts and seeds, especially Brazil and hickory nuts and sesame and sunflower seeds; dry beans, notably navy, soy, kidney, and lima; bitter and sweet chocolate; all varieties of molasses; curry powder; cocoa powder; caffeinefree ground coffee; tea; and dried yeast.

Table - 1
Copper Containing Proteins/Enzymes

1. Haemocyanin	-	present in blood of certain invertebrates like crab spider, snail and is involved in oxygen transport.
2. Haemocuprein	-	Copper protein compound found in red blood corpuscles. Also called erythrocuprein
3. Hepatocuprein	-	Copper protein complex present in liver
4. Cerebrocuprein	-	Present in human brain in the form of copper protein complex.
5. Ceruloplasmin	-	copper binding protein of the serum or plasma, functions in oxidation of plasma iron for the formation of transferrin-bound iron.
6. Cytochrome oxidase	-	functions in electron transport chain.
7. Superoxide dismutase	-	detoxifies free radicals.
8. Tyrosinase	-	involved in melanin production.
9. Dopamine ß hydroxylase	-	production of catecholamine.
10. Lysyl oxidase	-	crosslinking of collagen and elastin.

Besides these, other enzymes containing copper are Ascorbic acid oxidase, polyphenol oxidase, catalase, uricase, amine oxidases etc.

METABOLISM

Under normal conditions, copper is absorbed from the stomach and upper part of the small intestine and circulated in the blood loosely bound to albumin and passes on to the liver. The liver (main storage organ) concentrates the copper first in the cytosol and then in the mitochondria and finally in the nuclei, depending upon the dose and time of ingestion. It appears in the plasma in the form of ceruloplasmin. Copper is not readily excreted in the urine as it is largely bound to protein in the plasma. Most of the copper is lost in the faces through the intestine and a very small percentage may be excreted in urine.

DEFICIENCY

Nutritional deficiency has not been positively demonstrated in man but occurs in sheep causing anemia, abnormalities of skin, degeneration of nervous system and nephrosis. Copper has therefore been suggested to play a role in the body particularly to (i) in the metabolism of red cells (ii) regulating the oxidation-reduction enzymes of the tissues such as cytochrome system. Copper and iron metabolism appears to be related. The movement of iron from the tissues to the plasma results in copper deficiency with hypoferremia. Copper also helps in haemoglobin formation by releasing iron stores from the liver. Absorption of iron from the gastrointestinal tract is increased by the presence of copper. Copper is also found in Tyrosinase, an enzyme involved in converting tyrosine into melanin, the pigment responsible for the colour of the skin. Hence, absence of copper results in loss of hair colour and darkening of skin. Also copper is responsible for formation of aortic elastin and lack of it may cause aortic rupture, due to Lyoyl oxidase deficiency.

Table - 2
Estimated Safe and Adequate Daily Dietary Intakes of Copper

	Age (Years)	Copper (mg)
Infants	0-0.5	0.5-0.7
	0.5-1	0.7-1.0
Children and	1-3	1.0-1.5
adolescents	4-6	1.5-2.0
	7-10	2.0-2.5
	11+	2.0-3.0
Adults		2.0-3.0

SOURCE: Food and Nutrition Board, *Recommended Dietary Allowances*, 9th ed., Washington, D.C.: National Academy of Sciences, 1980, p.178.

Recent observations that there is reduced incorporation of labelled fatty acid into mitochondrial phospholipids in copper deficiency suggests either a direct participation of copper in phospholipid synthesis or that the low cytochrome oxidase activity affects the supply of ATP required for this process. Further study of this relationship is desirable in view of the frequency with which lesions are detectable in phospholipid-rich tissues during copper deficiency in many species.

Whether or not the copper proteins erythrocuprein, hepatocuprein, cerebrocuprein and neonatal hepatic mitochondrocuprein have metabolic functions other than as tissue stores of copper remains to be determined. A soluble copper protein of low molecular weight is present in liver, kidney and intestinal mucosa but is less well characterized.

The concentration of copper-bearing proteins of this type is apparently increased in cases of Wilson's disease in man and the quantity of copper bound in this form appears to be greatly affected by high tissue concentrations of zinc and by known antagonists of copper such as cadmium. There is some evidence to suggest that the antagonistic effect of molybdenum upon copper metabolism is achieved by increasing the extent of copper binding to tissue protein fractions.

The concentration of copper in the liver of the human infant is high at birth and then rapidly declines. The extent of redistribution of copper between the various copper proteins has not been characterized and the significance of any such changes during the development of copper deficiency in a human infant has not been determined.

The symptomatology of copper deficiency in farm livestock and experimental animals includes defects in collagen, elastin and wool keratin synthesis, diarrhoea and, when depletion is severe, the development of an anaemia resistant to iron therapy. The pattern of signs exhibited depends greatly upon the stage of growth and development at which depletion commences, and in the human infant, blood copper and ceruloplasmin determinations are not reliable indicators of copper status. Experimental studies indicate that assays of plasma amine oxidase activity and tissue cytochrome oxidase activity provide more satisfactory parameters for the detection of copper deficiency, but their possible value as diagnostic indices in man has not been investigated.

Copper deficiency of dietary origin has been detected in infants prematurely weaned on to cow's milk/cereal diets and in children rehabilitated from Kwashiorkor or marasmus on diets low in copper. In the fatal Menke's syndrome in human infants the copper content of tissues is low. In this syndrome there are degenerative changes in aortic elastin and changes in the skeletal metaphyses, in cerebral vascularity and in the composition of the hair similar to lesions reported in copper-deficient experimental animals and farm livestock. Studies on human biopsy material have clearly indicated defects in the activity of copper-dependent enzyme systems and an increased intake of copper has resulted in clinical improvement in all but neurological signs. It remains to be determined whether this syndrome is associated with a defect in copper accumulation during foetal development or is a post natal absorptive defect. This recent demonstration of disorders partially or wholly responsive to copper therapy should stimulate further survey and investigational work.

Copper is intimately involved in kinetic aspects of iron metabolism and haemopoiesis. The role of the copper enzyme ceruloplasmin in these processes is controversial and probably other roles exist but have not been adequately studied. It is probable that such investigations would be relevant both to a clearer understanding of tissue iron haemoglobin relationships and to the aetiology of haemosiderosis.

In farm livestock and experimental animals 'conditioned' copper deficiency is commonly associated with high dietary intakes of molybdenum, cadmium, zinc and a range of sulphides. Unidentified components of rapidly growing herbage also appear to have an adverse effect upon copper status. The relevance of these situations to the copper nutrition of man is unknown but should not be overlooked.

TOXICITY

Wilson's disease is associated with abnormalities in copper metabolism. Large amount of copper accumulates in tissues, particularly in liver and lenticular neucleus of the brain. This is due to the considerable increase in absorption of copper from the intestine. Large amount of copper in the unbound form is excreted in urine. This is an inborn error of human metabolism. The increased copper deposition in liver causes cirrhosis while in brain causes death of neurons and in kidney causes renal tubular damages. Sometimes copper accumulates in the cornea leading to a characteristic brown or green ring called the Kayser Fleischer ring.

EFFECTS ON PERINATAL DEVELOPMENTS

The important role of copper in perinatal development of mammals was first demonstrated when a disease affecting the developing foetus, could be prevented by administration of copper of these during pregnancy. Copper deficient sheep showed hemorrhagic underdeveloped brains, especially hypoplasia of the cerebellum. Copper deficiency in pregnant rats has also resulted in the birth of abnormal young. Newborn pups from copper deficient dams were hyperirritable with convulsive seizures after stimulation. Gross neural lesions were seen in the brain as well as enlarged and abnormal mitochondria. However, peroxidation of brain lipids was not increased despite subnormal activity of copper-zinc SOD.

Prenatal copper deficiency results in fatal death, early neonatal death, neurological abnormalities and a number of lesions which can be ascribed to the role of copper in lysyloxidase, the enzyme necessary for cross linking of normal elastin. These lesions affect the cardiovascular system, the lung (with abnormal development), skin and possible hair abnormalities as well as skeletal abnormalities related to impaired cross linking of collagen. Low copper content of tissues and low activity of the copper metalloenzymes cytochrome oxidase and copper-zinc SOD are other characteristics. The effects of prenatal copper deficiency are summarised in Table 3.

Table - 3
Effects of Prenatal Copper Deficiency

Fetal death	Early neonatal death
Neurological abnormalities	Imparied cross linking of elastin
Cardiovascular lesions	Aneurisms of aortic arch
Abnormal lung development	Skin abnormalities
Skeletal abnormalities	Hair abnormalities
Low copper content of tissue	Low activity of copper metalloenzymes
Cytochrome oxidase	Copper-zinc superoxide dismutase
Low copper content of tissues	Low activity of copper metalloenzymes
Cytochrome oxidase	Copper-zinc superoxide dismutase

4

SELENIUM

Selenium occurs along with sulphur in coal and the coal based thermal power plants release selenium as selenium oxides in to the atmosphere and solid waste (fly ash). In addition some soils also contain excess selenium, released from natural degradation of seleniferous rocks. The soils containing 5 mg/kg selenium or above are known as toxic soils or seleniferous soils. Generally selenium in soils is present in water-insoluble form. However, even soils having very low level of selenium (0.19 mg/kg) could produce vegetation containing toxic levels of selenium. Variation in the selenium content of vegetation could be due to the variation in the soil properties which control the adsorption of selenium and the nutrient mining power of plants.

Selenium exists in different compound forms in the soil the relative abundance of which depends on the soil pH.

Selenate compounds predominate over a wide range of pH. Whereas in the low pH or alkaline soils biselenite compounds and in high pH selenites are the major species. Elemental selenium or selinide occurs only at low-redox conditions. Both selenite and selenate are not so readily soluble in water. Dissolution and leaching of these soil salts by irrigation water is a primary source of selenium in ground water. Further, selenite is rapidly adsorbed on the soil while selenate is not adsorbed. In other words, selenate is ea00sily leached from the soil. The plants convert some of the selenium to organic selenium compounds which are volatile. The selenium content of plant species growing on seleniferrous soils is 4 to 170 times more than that of plants from non-seleniferrous soils. However, not all plants growing on selenium rich soils accumulate selenium. The amount of selenium accumulated varies from plant to plant.

Some of the plants known to accumulate selenium (not necessarily to lethal levels) in India are : wheat, rice, sugarcane, ratoon, peas, potato tubers, raddish, carrot, turnip and tomato. Garlic accumulates selenium to the highest level (30 mg/kg) while coriander, fenugreek. red pepper and turmeric contain slightly lower concentration of selenium.

METABOLISM

Different forms of selenium, selenites, selenates and seleniferrous compounds are absorbed from the gastrointestinal tract. The rate of absorption of these salts are rapid but selenides and elemental selenium are comparatively low and some organic selenium compounds are poorly absorbed.

Absorbed selenium is complexed with plasma proteins and is distributed to all tissues. Excretion of selenium is by faeces, urine and exhaled air depending on intake.

FUNCTION

Selenium when present in the diet above 5-15 ppm is highly toxic to animals. Selenium in small amounts may be essential factor in tissue respiration. Recently, a metabolically active selenium containing compound called factor 3 isolated from the yeast has been found to protect the liver against fatty infiltration and necrosis. The action of selenium may be related to vitamin E as the two substances appear to act synergestically in curing the hepatic disease, breast cancer and hypertension and certain muscle disorders induced in animals. Moreover, muscular distrophy in chicken (known as white muscle disease) can be prevented by selenium. It has also been shown that selenium is effective against Exudative Diathesis. The function of selenium involved is particularly that of a cofactor for enzymes related to cell oxidation. It is a component of glutathione peroxidase which protects the cell membrane.

DEFICIENCY

A daily intake of selenium of about 50-200 micrograms is advised. Deficiency symptoms appear if the intake is 10 μg or less per day. Selenium deficiency causes a number of diseases such as cancer, cardiovascular diseases and progressive muscular distrophy. Finnish scientists have reported that a correlation can be found between low levels of selenium in blood and ischemic heart disease. Smokers who run high risks of getting heart diseases also have low levels of selenium than non-smokers. In a very interesting report in the journal of Medicinal Chemistry (Aug.19, 1994), Dr. Will Taylor and his colleagues report that selenium plays a vital role in triggering the development of full blown AIDS. Human Immuno deficiency Virus (HIV) which causes AIDS contains at least four selenoproteins. These selenoproteins deplete selenium from the body. The infected cell is deficient in selenium and the virus spreads to other cells in search of selenium. Dr. Taylor's team suggest that supplementing selenium immediately in the diet of HIV- positive patients may restrict the disease.

Another important corelation found is that between vitamin E and selenium requirements of humans. It is reported that a proper combination of the two prevent aging. It is possible that a diet low in sodium and rich in carbohydrates, potassium, magnesium, calcium, zinc and selenium not only prevents aggravation of hypertension but might also cause significant reduction in blood pressure and its complications. A combination of vitamin A, E and selenium is reported to be beneficial in preventing even breast cancer.

In humans, it is now suggested that Keshan disease, a congestive cardiomyopathy with the pathological features of Keshan disease, associated with reduced erythrocyte and cardiac selenium and glutathione peroxide levels was noted in patients on home on total parenteral nutrition (TPN) unsupplemented by selenium for 4 years. Additional of selenium to the TPN solution corrected the symptoms within 1 week.

TOXICITY

Although selenium is essential in low concentrations to animals it is toxic if ingested in large amounts. This dual nature of selenium has estimulated investigations all over the world on the dietary requirements of selenium by humans as well as animals and plants. In buffalo calves 0.3 mg per kg body weight of selenium produces toxicity and may even result in death. Animals fed on selenium rich fodder show many type of symptoms, like development of cracks on the hooves followed by gradual detachment, peeling off of horns and loss of hair from the body and tail degeneration. The presence of high selenium in blood, hair and hooves (4 g/g, 28 g/g and 31 g/g respectively) confirm such selenium poisoning. The selenium content of hooves, blood and hair will be normally 42, 65 and 500 times lower in the health animals than the concentrations in affected animals. These types of affected animal are called 'alkali diseased animals' and are symptomised by lameness, degeneration of heart, liver and kidney. It is likely that selenium displaces sulfur in keratin, resulting in changes in hair, nails, hooves. There is also loss of hair from the body followed by degeneration of tail.

In human, toxicity of selenium occur through selenium dusts (e.g., selenium dioxide, selenium trioxide and certain halogen compounds that absorbs through lungs and skin.)

Selenium is neurotoxic, tetragenic, hepatotoxic and retards growth. It also causes muscle weakness, hepatic necrosis and infertility.

MECHANISM OF ACTION

Selenium is a metalloid with chemical properties somewhat similar to sulfur. Selenium may replace sulfur in cysteine and methionine in the body tissues if it is ingested over periods of time in sufficient quantity. This is the main mechanism of action for selenium poisoning.

Bromobenzene is used for treatment of removing selenium containing cysteine. The blood levels of selenium dropped in patients treated with bromobenzene and urinary excretion of selenium rose in the therapy. The selenium was excreted in the form of bromo mercapturic acid.

(Fig.1)

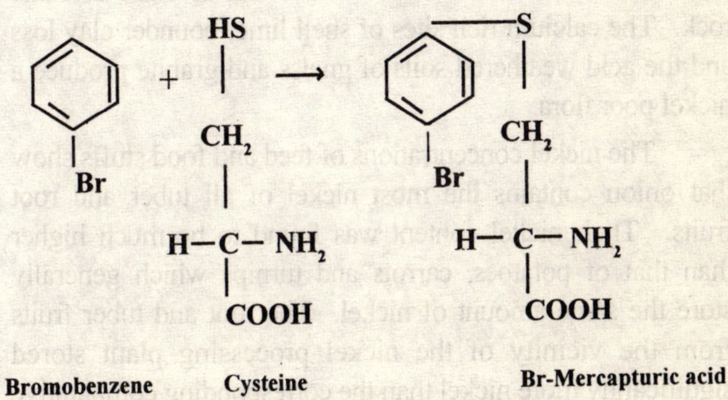

5

NICKEL

Nickel concentrations of feed and food stuffs is site specific and that the magnesium rich weather soils of the lower strata of new red sandstone and of keuper contain the most nickel, apart from those of slate and of basic volcanic rock. The calcium rich sites of shell lime, bounder clay loss and the acid weathered soils of gneiss and granite produce a nickel poor flora.

The nickel concentrations of feed and food stuffs show that onion contains the most nickel of all tuber and root fruits. Their nickel content was found to be much higher than that of potatoes, carrots and turnips which generally store the same amount of nickel. The root and tuber fruits from the vicinity of the nickel processing plant stored significantly more nickel than the corresponding comparative area.

It is seen that less nickel comes to human rations via animal products than via plant products, but still enough to cover the assumed requirement of 200 μg/kg dry matter of the ration. Generally, unprocessed meat is relatively nickel poor. The same is true for cardiac muscle, liver and kidney. Processed animal products have increased concentrations, sausage and canned products contain more nickel than the original material.

The toxicological manifestations of nickel depend on the form, level of exposure and mode of entry in the body. Nickel or nickel salts are relatively nontoxic when taken orally.

Nickel toxicity may occur through four different routes—

(1) oral intake,

(2) inhalation,

(3) parenteral administration,

(4) percutaneous absorption.

Abnormally high levels of dietary nickel are required to cause toxicity in humans. Nickel toxicity from parenteral administration is observed only in experimental conditions and therefore not a practical consideration for man. Nickel toxicity manifested by dermatitis is relatively common. Since many items in everyday use contains Nickel, this toxicity is always present. The most serious type is inhalation of nickel carbonyl which may however occur as a consequence of industrial accident. This includes dysnea, tachypnea, cyanosis, fever, vomiting, diarrhoea.

MECHANISM

Owing to its lipid solubility, nickel carbonyl is able to pass across cell membranes without metabolic alterations. The ability of Nickel Carbonyl to penetrate intracellularly is presumed to be responsible for its extreme toxicity decomposing within the cell to liberate cobalt and nickel, which is oxidised to Ni(II) by intracellular oxidation systems.

A different mechanism may be postulated for intracellular transport of insoluble inorganic nickel dust and nickel subsulfide (Ni_3S_2). After intramuscular injection these compounds are presumed to be deposited extracellularly and to dissolve slowly in the extracellular fluid and muscle autolysate.

Research on rats show that Nickel can inhibit RNA synthesis owing to impaired transport of RNA precursors across the nuclear membrane. Experiments show that manganese can inhibit the carcinogenicity of Nickel subsulfide by antagonising Nickel inhibition of RNA polymerase activity.

DEFICIENCY

In goats, mini-pigs, and rats, nickel poor rations resulted in decreased growth, with the growth expression dependent on the nickel level becoming significant only in the second generation. In goats, intrauterine nickel deficiency of mothers and their foetuses lead to significantly decreased birth sights. Together with growth depression, rate with a nickel poor ration showed anemia, which manifested itself in decreased haemoglobin and hematocrit values. The anemia was not removed by providing additional iron. In rats, the iron absorption rate was significantly decreased due to nickel deficiency. These results in rats proved true in several experiments. It was found that the haemoglobin and hematocrit value of the blood of nickel deficient goats after birth was significantly below the level of corresponding control animals, independent of the number of births.

Recently, parakeratosis like skin and hair diseases, which developed particularly during lactation and were to be seen at the udder of goats, occurred in pigs and goats with nickel deficiency and disturbed calcium metabolism. Changes in the epithelium of legs and hair could also be observed in hens and rats. The analysis of different parts of the body showed that nickel deficient animals were not only poor in nickel and calcium but also in zinc. These findings consistently prove to be the cause in both species.

The first indication of the importance of nickel for the microbiological increase production was shown when it was found that jack bean urease contained nickel at the active site. Nickel doses supplemented lead to promotion of growth and urease activity in different species of plants. The enzyme carbon monoxide dehydrogenase necessary for the oxidation of carbon monoxide into carbon dioxide is a nickel dependent enzyme as was shown in *Clostridium pasteuriauum*. Hence, nickel is essential for certain metabolic processes of bacteria and plants and that *via* them, it also influences the flora of the intestine. This is of particular importance for ruminants and species of animals with distinct appendix digestion (such as horses).

6

COBALT

A need for trace element was discovered when investigators found that it prevented a wasting disease among the cattle and sheep in certain localities in Australia and New Zealand. These studies were further reinforced by a similar ones for the same disease in Florida, Kenya, Scotland and England. Although deficiencies of this mineral have been found in cattle and sheep, they have not been produced in rats, rabbits or guinea pigs. However, there has been some evidence that cobalt will contribute to growth in rats and chicks.

Dietary cobalt is needed by ruminants for supplying the vitamin B_{12} where cobalt is the chief constituent. Sheep and cattle raised in Australia and other parts of the world on cobalt deficient pastures develop a disease once thought to be a simple cobalt lack, now known to be a vitamin B_{12} deficiency. The vitamin contains about 4 percent cobalt.

Bacteria in the rumer of animals synthesize the vitamins. When the diet contains enough cobalt and the vitamin is then absorbed. When the fodder is deficient in cobalt, the vitamin lack is evident.

In man this synthesis occurs in the colon where absorption is minimal, if any. Therefore, to be of nutritional value to the human being, cobalt must be ingested as the preformed vitamin. The need for cobalt other than as vitamin B_{12} is not known. The usual diet supplies from 5 to 8 μg cobalt, comparatively little is absorbed. Small amounts are found in the red blood cells and plasma and some storage takes place in the liver, kidney, pancreas and spleen. Excretion is largely in the urine. Because erythropoesis is improved when cobalt is administrated in therapeutic doses, the mineral sometimes is used for the treatment of some anemias. However, cobalt therapy has produced unpleasant side effects in some instances and permanent benefit has not always followed treatment. Besides anemia, deficiency of cobalt causes stunted growth. Excess of cobalt, on the other hand, causes coronary failure and thyroid disfunctions.

7

ZINC

Zinc is widely distributed in oysters, seafood, liver, wheat, germ, and yeast. Green leafy vegetables, fruits, whole grains, meat and fish are good sources of zinc.

The human body contains about 2 gm of zinc, comparatively large amounts are found in the liver, voluntary muscle and bone. The iris retina and lens of the eye and the corneal epithelium are high in this mineral, as are the prostate gland and its secretions and spermatozoa. Zinc is found in the teeth, especially in the outer surface of the enamel. The insulin molecule contains about 0.3 percent zinc.

DEFICIENCY

Zinc deficiency in human subjects has been reported to occur in conditions in which there is an increased requirement of zinc, e.g. infants and children during the rapid growth age period and women who are pregnant and lactating (Table-1). The recommended dietary allowances for zinc in infants, adolescents, and pregnant women are relatively high and unlikely to be met on an ordinary diet.

Table - 1
Causes of Zinc Deficiency

1. Nutritional	5. Chronic renal disease
2. Alcohol	6. Latrogenic
3. Liver disease	7. Genetic disorders
4. Malabsorption	(a) Acrodermatitis enteropathica
	(b) Sickle cell disease

Predominant use of cereal proteins by the majority of the world population is a very important predisposing factor for zinc deficiency. The availability of zinc in such diet is very poor because of the high phosphate and phytate content. Zinc deficiency has been reported to occur in patients with malabsorption syndrome. In such cases, zinc deficiency is likely to occur in association with other deficiencies.

Hyperzincuria, over an extended period, may lead to zinc depletion. Urinary excretion of zinc appears to vary with the amount of element bound to the plasma amino acid pool. Thus, in those conditions where histidine and cysteine increase in the plasma, one would expect to find hyperzincuria. Conditions associated with hypercatabolic state, such as surgery, burns, multiple injuries, major fractures, diabetes mellitus, protein deprivation and starvation, usually exhibit hyperzincuria.

Proteinuria and use of chelating agents such as penicillamine will also result in excessive zinc loss in the urine. Severe deficiency of zinc resulting from penicillamine therapy in a patient with Wilson's disease has been reported. Hyperzincuria has also been observed following chlorothiazide administration. Thus, hypertensive patients on long-term therapy with chlorothiazide should be monitored for zinc deficiency. Glucagon, too, is known to cause hyperzincuria.

Proteinuria and use of chelating agents such as penicillamine will also result in excessive zinc loss in the urine. Severe deficiency of zinc resulting from penicillamine therapy in a patient with Wilson disease is found.

Patients with chronic liver disease, nephrotic syndrome and sickle cell disease are known to have hyperzincuria. It has recently been shown that several of the clinical manifestations of sickle cell disease and chronic liver disease are indeed due to zinc deficiency, and zinc supplementation corrects these manifestations.

At present, two genetic disorders, acrodermatitis enteropathica (AE) and sickle cell disease, are known to be associated with zinc deficiency. All the clinical manifestations of AE seem to be reversible with zinc supplementation. In sickle cell disease, clinical manifestations such as growth retardation, hypogonadism in males, abnormal dark adaptation, hyperammonemia, general lethargy, and poor appetite appear to be related to a deficiency of zinc.

Severe zinc deficiency in patients receiving long-term total parenteral nutrition without zinc supplementation has been reported by several investigators. Symptoms are similar to those seen in AE and include skin rashes, alopecia, diarrhoea and depression. The onset of symptoms, usually 5 to 10 weeks after the start of total parenteral nutrition, is related to the severity of zinc depletion in the patient.

CLINICAL MANIFESTATIONS

Growth retardation, hypogonadism in males, poor appetite, mental lethargy and skin changes were the classical features of chronically zinc deficient subjects from the Middle East as reported in the early sixties. Recently abnormal visual adaptation to the dark in alcoholic cirrhotics has been related to a deficiency in zinc. It is proposed that the effect of zinc on the retina may be mediated by an enzyme, retinene reductase, which is known to be zinc dependent.

It is likely that some of the clinical features of cirrhosis of the liver, such as loss of body hair, testicular hypofunction, poor appetite difficulty in wound healing and night blindness may be related to the secondary zinc deficient state in this disease. 'Featal alcohol syndrome' is characteristic of pre and postnatal growth deficiency, microphaly, short palpebral fissures, epicanthal folds, small jaw, joint deformaties cardiac, renal and genitalia anomalies. In sickle cell disease, delayed onset of puberty and hypogonadism in males, characterised by decreased facial, pubic and axillary hair, short stature, low body weight, rough skin and poor appetite have been noted and related to a secondary zinc deficient state. The dermatological manifestations of severe zinc deficiency include progressive bullous-pustupar dermatitis of the extremities and the oral, anal and genital areas combined with infection with *Candida albicans*. Neuropsychiactric signs of severe zinc deficiency include irritability, emotional disorders, tremors and occasional cerebellar ataxia. The patients generally have stunted growth and males exhibit hypogonadism. Zinc therapy has been shown to produce remarkable improvements and is considered to be life saving measure in these subjects.

Table - 2

Manifestations of Zinc Deficiency

Mild	Moderate	Severe
Oligospermia	Growth retardation	Bullous-pustular dermatitis
Weight loss	Hypogonadism in males	Alopesia
Pyperammonemia	Skin changes	Diarrhea
	Poor appetite	Emotional disorders
	Mental lethargy	Weight loss
	Delayed wound healing	Intercurrent infections
	Taste abnormalities	Hypogonadism in males
	Abnormal dark adaptation	Fatal if treated

FUNCTIONS

Major functions of zinc in human and animal metabolism appear to be enzymatic. There are over 70 metalloenzymes known to require zinc for their functions. Zinc enzymes are known to participate in a wide variety of metabolic processes. The metal is present in several dehydrogenases, aldolases, peptidases and phosphates.

Ribonucleic acid (RNA) and Deoxyribonucleic acid (DNA) polymerases are known to be zinc metalloenzymes, Deoxythymidine Rinase is also zinc dependent. In addition, the catabolic rate of RNA appears to be regulated by zinc, in asmuch as the activity of RNase is known to increase as a result to zinc deficiency. Zinc is required for all phases of the cell cycle. This is undoubtedly related to its vital role in DNA synthesis.

Zinc has a vital role in vitamin A metabolism. Zinc may stimulate the release of vitamin A from the liver into the blood. Moreover, zinc containing retinal reductase participates in the regeneration of rhodopsin in the eye following light exposure.

Zinc occurs in many metalloproteins like carboxypeptidase A, cytoplasmic superoxide dismutase, carbonic anhydrase, alcohol dehydrogenase etc. Carboxypeptidase A is present in erythrocytes and in other parts of the body and aids in carbon dioxide transport. Carbonic anhydrase, on the other hand, is involved in the breakdown of peptides into amino acids in the intestinal tract. Alcohol dehydrogenase is a zinc protein and continued use of alcohol may alter the enzyme in some way leading to its degradation and to zincuria. Much of the element is excreted in the urinary tract.

Zinc is a constituent of crystalline insulin although zinc free insulin preparations are available. The zinc content of the pancreas in diabetic patients is about one half of the normal amount indicating that the element may be concerned with the storage and utilisation of insulin.

High levels of zinc in ovary, uterus and vagina during proestrus and estrous and in uterus and vagina of ovariectomized estrogen treated rats have been correlated to increased levels of estrogen. Zinc is also required for timely uptake and processing of estrogen and above all, both estrogen and progesterone receptors are zinc metalloproteins. Zinc deficiency has been incriminated in abnormal ovarial development and functions (such as hyperhaploidy, hypohaploidy increased atresia, induced accumulation of coarse granules of phospholipids, triglycerides and cholesterol in cells of granulose, theca interna, externa and interstitium, disruption of estrous cycle and infertility.

Under the influence of increased estrogen in proestrous or estrogen treated ovariectomized rats, the estrogen and progesterone receptors are increased in target organs, i.e., ovary, uterus and vagina and the increased estrogen transport into the cells in turn leads to increased DNA replication, RNA transcription, protein synthesis, cell division etc. Further, since estrogen and progesterone receptors and several enzymes of steroidogenesis, gene expression, DNA replication, RNA transcription and protein synthesis are Zn metallo protein, hence, an increased demand of Zinc in the ovary, uterus and vagina during proestrous and estrous and in ovariectomised-estrogen treated rats is evident. Decreased concentration of the element during metaestrous and diestrous has been correlated to decreased concentration of estrogen and hence decreased synthesis of nucleic acids and cell division.

Zinc is localised in high amounts in cells responsible for production, storage and release of hormones of the anterior pituitary (100 μg/g dry weight of pituitary) of female rats. At supra physiological concentrations (100 mg) Zinc reduces prolactin synthesis and secretions and increases LH secretions. Increased plasma zinc levels are reported to cause a fall in prolactin level in human beings. Also clinical states with tendency to zinc deficiency are also associated with a tendency to hyperpolactamia. Thus, it is hypothesized that prolactin regulates uptake and distribution of zinc and that suppresses prolactin in closure of a negative feed back regulatory loop. Therefore in reduced supply of zinc, high levels of prolactin and decreased levels of LH are evident. This way further add to the suppression of ovarian functions.

Hence, zinc deficiency may lead to (1) reduction in energy, protein intake and in GnRM secretions by hypothalamus and eventually leads to decreased LH and FSH levels, (2) increased synthesis and/or secretions of prolactin, (3) reduced output of estrogen, and (4) eventually leads to arrest of ovulation and increased atresia of follicles.

ZINC REQUIREMENT DURING INFANCY

The infant is born without zinc body stores. Tissue concentration are similar to those of adults. Therefore, infants become rapidly dependent on a dietary source. Breast fed infants receive 0.7 to 5.0 mg/day of zinc. Levels of zinc in human milk decline after 2 months of lactation and may fall below 1.0 mg. Although there are not enough data to state the requirement of infant, it has been shown that 3 mg during the first six months and 5 mg during the second six months has given beneficial effects. Bioavailability studies indicate that human milk has 59.2 per cent, cow's milk 42 per cent and commercial milk 26-39 per cent of zinc.

Table - 3
Recommended Daily Dietary Allowances for Zinc

	Age	Weight		Height		Zinc
	(Years)	(kg)	(lb)	(cm)	(in)	(mg)
Infants	0.0 - 0.5	6	13	60	24	3
	0.5 - 1.0	9	20	71	28	5
Children	1 - 3	13	29	90	35	10
	4 - 6	20	44	112	44	10
	7 - 10	28	62	132	52	10
Males	11 - 14	45	99	157	62	15
	15 - 18	66	145	176	69	15
	19 - 22	70	154	177	70	15
	23 - 50	70	154	178	70	15
	51+	70	154	178	70	15
Females	11 - 14	46	101	157	62	15
	15 - 18	55	120	163	64	15
	19 - 22	55	120	163	64	15
	23 - 50	55	120	163	64	15
	51+	55	120	163	64	15
Pregnant						+5
Lactating						+10

SOURCE: Food and Nutrition Board, *Recommended Dietary Allowances*, 9th ed. (Washington, D.C.: National Academy of Sciences, 1980).

8

MANGANESE

Manganese occurs in plant and animal tissues and the ordinary daily diet contains around 4 mg manganese that is enough for human being. Hence, manganese deficiency is rarely found in man. However, manganese is considered important for good nutrition. The main dietary sources of manganese are plants, with tea, coffee, blueberries, bran, dry legumes and nuts being particularly rich of around 200 mg/kg. Among the poor sources are meat, poultry, fish egg, dairy products and non leafy vegetables. Cow milk contains about 0.3 mg/litre and egg 0.01-0.02 mg per egg.

DEFICIENCY

Manganese activates a number of enzymes including arginase, leucine amino peptidase, bone phosphatase, phosphoglucomutase, hexokinase, isocitric dehydrogenase, pyrophosphates, pyruvate decarboxylase, cholinesterase and a variety of enzymes active in oxidative phosphorylation. In animals, deficiency results in retarded growth, lessened reproductive capacity and nerve disorders. In poultry, lack of manganese results in bone disorders known as perosis. This disease is aggravated by lack of choline in the diet and is known that manganese and choline are both involved in fat metabolism and skeletal development. Manganese has also been shown to inactivate pherentasin, a vasoconstrictive compound which is a factor in hypertension. Manganese plays a significant role in synthesis and deposition of proteoglycans in many tissues including bones, by helping in glycosyl transferase activity. Deficiency may lead to bone deformities in chicks and lameness in pigs.

In humans, manganese deficiency during prenatal life may lead to congenital ataxia, characterised by inco-ordination, lack of equilibrium and retraction of the head. The most crucial test for this condition is swimming. When the off- spring of manganese deficient animals are placed in a tank of water, they are unable to keep their heads above the surface and will drown if not removed. The ataxia has been found to be due to abnormal development of the otoliths of the inner ear. The otoliths, which are calcified structures in the vestibular portion of the inner ear and eye necessary for normal vestibular function or balance are composed of small crystalline otolithic embedded in a mucopolysaccharide rich amorphous otolithic matrix. The basic biochemical defect leading to abnormal development of the otoliths in manganese deficiency appears to be depressed synthesis of mucopolysaccharides. This is demonstrated by depressed uptake of sulphur in the otholithic matrix of manganese deficient fetuses. Manganese function biochemically as a cofactor for a number of enzymes. The particular growth of manganese dependent enzymes related to the synthesis of mucopolysaccharides are the glycosyl transferase enzymes, which catalyses the transfer of glycosyl in the first step of glycoseminoglycan and glycoprotein synthesis. It was also demonstrated that manganese deficient animals have a lower than normal activity of these enzymes; that leads eventually to the congenital ataxia produced by maternal dietary manganese deficiency.

Another major effect of prenatal manganese deficiency is on the skeletal, where offsprings are apparent by birth and are characterised by a disproportionate growth with short, thick long bones and domed skull. All of the manifestations of these skeletal abnormalities can be explained by abnormal synthesis of mucopolysaccharides. It is believed that manganese in the glycosyl transferase is at the basis of these skeletal defects as well as in the inner ear defects. A wide range of enzymes which mediate phosphate group transfer are activated by manganese *in vitro.* These are non-specific effects often shared by magnesium and their biological significance remains doubtful. Probably more relevant to the essential functions of manganese is the observation that chondroitin sulphate synthesis is impaired in manganese deficient rats. It has been suggested that the enzymes sensitive to manganese depletion may be those concerned with the utilization of UDP galactose as intermediates during synthesis.

Defects in acid mucopolysaccharide synthesis are detectable during manganese deficiency in several species of experimental animals. Particular attention has been paid to faulty development of epiphyseal cartilage and the otolithic membrane which arises from failure to incorporate sulphate into mucopolysaccharides. Congenital ataxia in some strains of manganese deficient mice and guinea pigs appears to be a consequence of defective otolith formation during foetal development. There are clear indications that the incidence of this lesion is genetically determined; controversy exists as to whether the defect arises during absorption of manganese from the gut. The possible relationship of suboptimal manganese status to defects of mucopolysaccharide synthesis in man does not appear to have been investigated. Such an investigation may be particularly valuable if there appears to be a genetic component in the incidence of such disorders.

Ultrastructural abnormalities associated with a reduced oxygen uptake have been detected in liver mitochondria from manganese-deficient mice. The biochemical origin of this lesion is unknown. An impaired glucose tolerance in manganese-deficient experimental animals may be associated with observed changes in pancreatic islet structure. This situation has not so far been demonstrated in man. Experimental studies suggest that manganese deficiency may decrease conception in rats, and increase the proportion of stillbirths and abortions. The pathology and biochemistry of these situations need further study.

Suggestions that disturbances of manganese metabolism exist in rheumatoid arthritis and disseminated lupus erythematosus in man are not yet convincing and require further investigation. An interference with manganese metabolism may be associated with the use of hydralazine for the treatment of hypertension in man since remission of the signs of toxicity occurs in experimental animals when manganese supplements are given.

9

ALUMINIUM

Aluminium is the most abundant metal on earth's crust. In modern civilisation accumulation of aluminium in human body as well as in plants and in aquatic animals cannot be prevented. The source of aluminium contamination occurs (1) due to acid rain that reaches earth's crust and mix with ground and surface water, (2) this water is taken up by plants and aquatic animals and finally by herbivorous animals, and (3) humans accumulate aluminium from these animals, plants and also aquatic animals. The aluminium content of important food materials are given below:

Aluminium Content (Microgm/gm)

Natural cheese - 15.7	Tea bag - 1280
Processed cheese - 297	Tomato sauce - 0.10
Baking powder - 23,000	Cocoa - 40

Besides these, aluminium is excreted from aluminium utensils during cooking, especially when tomato sauce or other acidic agents are used during cooking. Tomato sauce contains about 0.1 μg/g aluminium but this rises up to 57.1 μg/gm aluminium when cooked in aluminium utensils. Aluminium also comes from antacids that contains aluminium hydroxide gel. Other pharmaceutical products also contains aluminium hydroxide type of complexes. The aluminium foil placed on some sweets or beetles may be a constant source of aluminium in food. Bakery products as backing powder contains aluminium in the form of aluminium sodium phosphate.

TOXICITY

Aluminium is neither essential nor beneficial. Adult human bears most of the aluminium in the lungs from inhalation. Following absorbtion, the highest concentration is found in the brain. Imparied kidney function reduces body's ability to clear aluminium. Aluminium toxicity can produce angular deformities of bone osteoporosis, dysfunction of liver, kidney and lungs, amyotropic lateral sclerosis or Alzheimer's disease, a type of presenile dementia like neuronal degeneration. Increase of aluminium content of human plasma from 0.005 ppm to 0.25 ppm leads to the following disorders:

(i) a type of anaemia which does not respond to iron therapy,

(ii) osteodystrophy of the bone which becomes susceptible to fracture and pain at joints, and

(iii) adverse neurological condition affecting speech and memory, eventually leading to dementia.

EFFECT ON AQUATIC LIFE

Due to natural weathering process aluminium and silicon finds their way from lithosphere into the hydrosphere where both are present at ppb and ppm levels respectively. Ocean water is weakly alkaline with a pH of around 8, where aluminium and silicon combine to form the stable hydroxyalumino silicates. At lower pH they break down to hydrated aluminium ion. In some industralised regions, the nitrogen dioxide and sulphur dioxide present in the air forms the acid rain (with pH as low as 4 sometime) that causes acidity of lakes and rivers in that region. Such acidic water helps to solubilise more aluminium from the rocks and soil into the water and maintain it in the solution in the form of aluminium hydroxides.

Aluminium is well known to be toxic to plants, fish and aquatic animals. When plants are grown in acidic soil, the readily available aluminium causes severe damage to the root system and retard growth. Fish in acidic water having 0.12-0.25 ppm aluminium shows total damage of gill structure leading to impaired respiration and loss of ability to maintain osmoregulatory balance.

MECHANISM OF ACTION

The adverse effects of aluminium on biological system are due to it's physico-chemical characteristics such as great preference of aluminium ion for ligands such as phosphate in membranes, DNA, ATP etc., and in this respect it's affinity is several orders of magnitude greater than that of some biologically essential metals like magnesium and calcium and also because ligand replacement in aluminium species is 10^4-10 times than these two metals. This higher affinity and slower exchange rate lead to significantly different biological consequences. Replacement of aluminium bound to a biological ligand is comparatively disfavoured both thermodynamically and kinetically. Replacement of magnesium from enzymes by aluminium causes deactivation and thus adversely affect important biochemical reactions which are dependent on these enzymes like kinases, polymerases, phosphatases etc.

EFFECT ON HUMAN BRAIN

Aluminium is present in the brain tissue of mammals at concentration between 1 and 2 µg/g dry wt. The toxic range for aluminium appears to be between 4 and 8 µg/dry wt of brain for cat and rabbit. Rats and mice are relatively resistance to the toxic effects of aluminium and do not develop a progressive encephalopathy. Aluminium has two unusual effects upon the central nervous system. This metal induces a slowly progressive encephalopathy, in which an early stage is characterised by a progressive learning memory deficit and certain neurons in the brains of affected animals exhibit a cytoplasmic accumulation of 10nm filaments called neurofibrillary degeneration. It causes relatively selective damage to the neuronal substrate responsible for learning memory performance.

It is to be expected that among animal species, the delayed, progressive aluminium-induced-encephalopathy is always associated with the morphological change of neurofibrillary degeneration, atleast in some cells. Species such as rats and mice developed neither a progressive encephalopathy nor neurofibriallary degeneration in response to the intracranial application of soluble aluminium salts. While the cellular disorder responsible for aluminium neurotoxicity remains unknown, it is expected that this highly reactive element would interact with several biological systems. Further, the various hydrated states and the ligand to which this element is bound may also alter the toxicity. In a variety of system, it has been noted that aluminium accumulates upon cellular nuclei. While intranucler accumulation of aluminium was initially demostrated by the use of the histochemical stain morin, this finding has recently been confirmed by atomic spectroscopy and the electron probe.

The conclusion that virtually all the aluminium is intranuclear is based on two arguments. In human brain, cerebral cortical nuclei, there are approximately 700 µg aluminium per gm deoxyribonucleic acid (DNA). Based on the assumption that all the aluminium is associated with DNA and the dry weight is approximately 20 per cent of the wet weight of brain, it is possible to predict the concentration of aluminium to be expected in whole neocortex and expressed as µg/gm dry wt. It has been shown *in vitro* that there are interactions of aluminium with DNA as demonstrated by thermal denaturation, circular dichroism and fluorescent bindings. *In vitro* experiments also indicates that aluminium reduces ribonucleic acid (RNA) synthesis.

The role of aluminium in human disease has also recently being explored and cannot be considered as established. The two most important human diseases in which aluminium has been implicated as a toxic factor are **dialysis encephalophathy** and **Alzheimer's disease**. These two conditions however defer markedly. In dialysis encephalopathy there is no histophathology. The aluminium levels in the tissue are very high, ranging between 10 to 20 times the normal levels. The aluminium is localised in the cytoplasm. Unlike the animal modes with a progressive encepalophathy, in which aluminium is localised intranuclear, the intranuclear aluminium concentration in dialysis dementia is lower than normals. In this condition, the primary disorder is renal failure and aluminium accumulates in all body tissue including the brain. Therefore the condition may be considered an aluminium overload condition, in which the brain is initially normal and is able to detoxify a large aluminium load. In the second disorder, Alzheimer's disease, there are several histopathological changes including neurofibrillary degeneration and senile plaques. However, other major histopathological findings of Alzheimer's disease including neuritic plaques with amyloid chores, granulovascular degeneration and amyloid angiopathy cannot be explained by the known neurotoxic effects of aluminium. Furthermore, in Alzheimer's disease, brain aluminium is only moderately elevated and the increase is patchy in distribution. The other tissues of the body are normal in aluminium content and one must consider the possibility that underline brain disease has altered the brain permeability or binding of aluminium and have allowed aluminium to accumulate. What is remarkable is however, that aluminium accumulates intranuclear and in approximately same ratio as is found in the other toxic aluminium encephalopathy in cats.

10

FLUORINE

Fluoride is present in minute amounts in nearly every human tissue but is found primarily in the skeleton and teeth, the organs contain more fluoride than do other soft tissues. Among the richer food source of animal origin are gelatin, the organs, seafoods and infant foods which contain bone meal. Cow's milk content may vary from 0.09 to 0.32 parts per million (ppm), cheese from 0.16 to 1.31 ppm. In plant foods the fluoride content varies accordingly to environmental conditions, among these are the type of soil, direction and intensity of prevailing winds and use of fertilisers and sprays which contain fluoride. Green leafy vegetables are specially susceptible to air borne fluoride, spinach containing 0.1 to 28.3 ppm. Fruits contain little unless sprayed with a fluoride compound. It has been estimated that an adult may secure 0.5 to 1.0 mg fluoride daily from his food.

FUNCTION

Interest in fluoride was aroused when it was found that this element present naturally in large amounts in the drinking water of certain localities, caused mottled tooth enamel and that this condition could be controlled by limiting the amount of the mineral to about 1.5 ppm. With 1 ppm or less in the water supply, the mottling was controlled but susceptibility to dental caries increased. This effect on tooth decay is evident especially during the time the teeth are forming.

The mechanism of this action is being studied. It has been shown that fluoride combines chemically with hydroxyapatite to form fluorapatite whose crystals are larger and more perfect in form. This in turn, results in reduced surface area and solubility. The outer layers of enamel have a higher fluoride content than the inner layers. Also, the fluoride content of the teeth and bones closely parallels the fluoride content of the water supply. These facts probably are related to the resistance of teeth to caries. Hence, addition of fluoride to water supply is advocated by public health authorities as a safe, inexpensive and effecient way to reduce dental caries. In places where the fluoride content in the water supply is low, sodium fluoride may be applied directly to the teeth. This tropical treatment should be started in preschool years and continued at regular intervals throughout the period of tooth formation.

Fluoride can reduce the incidence of dental caries. This is because Fluoride suppresses sugar metabolism by bacteria making enamel more resistance to acid and stimulates remineralization of the teeth. As mentioned earlier, a fluoridated water supply is important in prevention of dental caries. Other approaches to ensuring adequate fluoride intake that are under investigation all over the world include sodium fluoride capsules that can be chewed and swallowed, the use of aerosol that causes fluoride-containing organisms to adhere to the teeth and enhances fluoride uptake by the plaque and enamel and the use of a small devide attached to the teeth that releases fluoride at a predetermined rate for at least 6 months.

The role of fluoride in prenatal development is poorly understood at present. Some questions have existed over the past 50 years about the degree of fluoride transport across the placenta. Should it cross the placenta, question still remains about its value in the development of caries resistant permanent teeth. Development of the primary dentition begins at 10-12 weeks of pregnancy. From the sixth to ninth months of pregnancy, the first four permanent molars and eight of the permanent incisors begin to form. Thus 32 of the ultimate teeths are forming and developing during human pregnancy. Since there is no indication that color of the teeth is adversely affected and some evidence that caries resistance and morphologic characteristic are improved, prenatal fluoride supplementation may be justified. However, this issue is highly controversial and to date formal support for routine prenatal fluoride supplementation has not been voiced by an established medical or dental organisation. Fluorine has only recently been found to be an essential nutrient for growth in the rat. Diets low in fluorine also produce both anaemia and impaired fertility in female mice. These observations need to be confirmed, particularly in view of the fact that the suggested optimum intake of the element for growth is similar to that known to induce mild dental fluorosis. The nature of the essential role fulfilled by fluorine is unknown.

Many aspects of fluorine metabolism require investigation. Suggestions that much of the 'bound' fluorine present in human plasma is in a form unique to man should be investigated and the component identified. Both the relationship between dietary intake and the fluorine content of blood and urine and the relationship between sketetal content of fluorine and susceptibility to osteoporosis should be examined further.

The mechanism whereby high intakes of calcium adversely affect fluorine absorption is not known. Whether or not this antagonistic effect also applies to organic forms of fluorine present in diets requires particular attention. Much more information on the fluorine content of human and animal food is required, much of the past data appears questionable because of analytical inadequacies.

There is no general agreement on how fluorine, at concentrations of about 1 ppm in drinking water, reduces dental caries. No satisfactory explanation exists for apparent population differences in susceptibility to fluorosis of the dental enamel. Metabolic abnormalities resulting in the development of lesions in bone, joints and ligaments following an excessive intake of fluorine are not understood. The reasons for marked species difference in fluorine tolerance are unknown.

11

ARSENIC

Arsenic is widely distributed in plant and animal tissues. It is found in soil water and air. It is found in rocks and soils ranging from 1-100 ppm. It is also found in ground water and may cause toxicity when reached .5-1.0 mg/litre. It may be accumulated in the basic and needles of plants, and in many fishes and shellfish. It is also used as feed and additives for poultry.

TOXICITY

The general pattern of toxicity depends on oxidation state:

AsH_3, As^{3+}, As^{5+} RAs-X.

The general toxicity of Arsenic are (1) direct inhibition of cellular respiration, (2) mutagenic effects, (3) haemolysis.

(a) *Arsine gas* (AsH_3) causes rapid hemolysis and subsequent renal damage that may persist for years. One person suffers from nausea, headache, signs of shock anemia, hemoglobinuria and coppery skin pigmentation.

(b) *Arsenite* (As^{3+}) is absorbed from the GI tract and accumulates to a high level in tissues.

(c) *Arsenate* (As^{5+}) is probably the common environment form of inorganic arsenic.

(d) The *organoarsenicals* (RAs-X) like arsanilic acid causes toxicity to liver and kidney.

MECHANISM OF ACTION —

All arsenates causes inhibition of cellular respiration.

Arsenate

It is known as uncoupler of mitochondrial oxidative phosphorylation. The mechanism by which this occurs is thought to be related to competitive arsenate substitution for inorganic phosphate with subsequent formation of an unstable arsenate ester that spontaneously decomposes. This process is called arsenolysis.

Arsenate is also a well known tetratogen and has one ability to substitute for phosphate in some cellular processes, specially in DNA chain.

Arsenite

It causes inhibition of TCA cycle and some major enzymes like pyruvate oxidase, $NADH_2$ oxidase. It reacts with disulphydryl lipoic acid to cause accumulation of pyruvate in blood. Inhibition of pyruvate oxidation leads to decreased mitochondrial respiration.

Organoarsenicals

It produce toxicity like inorganic arsenite reacting with SH group of enzymes, particularly to those involved in cellular respiration.

Arsine gas

It produces hemolysis by inhibiting proteins responsible for maintenance of the osmotic balance within red cells. There is also a decreased glutathione content in these cells that may cause lysis.

Arsenic have been reported to have antagonistic interactions with Selenium. It decreases retention of Selenium and causes increased excretion from liver into the bile.

Management

The reasons for arsenic contamination of groundwater in different parts of the world is not very clear. It is difficult to state whether this is due to hydrological imbalance either due to heavy groundwater withdrawal for irrigation or seasonal water level fluctuations. Hence, it is essential to carry on extensive scientific study of sub-surface geology of the affected areas by government agencies in collaboration with various experts in the field so that the actual reason for high arsenic contamination of ground water could properly be known and long term corrective measures could be taken.

Skin pigmentation and de-pigmentation are not late manifestations of chronic arsenic toxicity but the early manifestation of the clinical problem. Many such people do not progress to more severe manifestations like liver fibrosis, respiratory distress due to chronic bronchitis or intestinal lung disease, peripheral neuritis, swelling of the legs or hand, defect of hearing or vision and so on. Detection of high level of arsenic in hair and nails in a person does not mean he is suffering from chronic arsenicosis. He is at a potential risk of developing skin cancer or cancer of internal organs. It should also be noted that drinking a glass or two of arsenic contaminated groundwater by a school child or person in a sweetmeat shop will not lead to the development of chronic arsenic toxicity. This is because the biological half time for urinary excretion of inorganic arsenic is 3-5 days. Chronic toxicity develops only when the arsenic contaminated water is taken continuously for a prolonged period.

Though a large number of people are suspected to be suffering from the menace of chronic arsenic toxicity, few physicians are conversant with the treatment of the problem. Though a few drugs are recommended to remove arsenic from the body, their role in curing the manifestations of the disease still require critical appraisal from clinical study. Current mode of management of non-cancer manifestations of chronic arsenic toxicity rests on asking the people to stop drinking arsenic contaminated water, to take high protein diet and to treat with drugs to ameliorate the symptoms which a patient presents to the doctor.

12

MAGNESIUM

Food rich in magnesium (over 100 mg per 100 gm) are cocoa and chocolate, nuts, whole grain products, soybeans, dried beans and peas and beat greens. Those with moderate content (25 to 75 mg per 100 gm) include most fish, most green vegetables, bananas, corn potatoes, dried fruits and hard cheese. Among the foods relatively poor in magnesium (under 25 mg per 100 gm) are refined grain products, eggs, and most fruits, vegetables, meats and dairy products. It has been seen that subtropical fruits such as avocados, bananas, figs, mangoes, papayas and pineapples contain higher magnesium values than citrus fruits and melons.

Cooking, specially boiling, results in magnesium losses. The presence of phytic acid in whole grains interferes with absorption of the mineral. It has been found that amount of dietary magnesium needed may depend on other dietary components. High protein, calcium, vitamin-D, phytates and alcohol tend to impede retention of magnesium or to increase its requirement, especially when intake is below 6 mg per kg per day. The FNB has set 350 mg per day as the allowance for the adult man, 300 mg for the adult woman. The RDA for preadolescents and adolescents vary with age. They are 300 to 400 mg for boys and 300 to 360 mg for girls. During pregnancy and lactation 450 mg per day are recommended. For infants and children, the allowances are based on the magnesium content of milk. This is about 4 mg per 100 ml human milk, 12 mg per 100 ml cow's milk.

DEFICIENCY

Symptoms of magnesium deficiency have been noted in human beings as well as in animals. Experimental work on animals has shown that a diet devoid of magnesium results in marked vasodilatation, necrotic changes, hyperirritability, convulsive seizures, and eventually death. On diets marginally deficient in magnesium, symptoms were less severe.

Similar symptoms have been observed in man. The resulting disease is like hypocalcemic tetany but shows low serum magnesium levels instead of low calcium levels. In human beings the tetany and low serum levels are associated with alcoholism, diabetes, kwarshiorkor, parathyroid disease, and malabsorption syndromes. Surgical patients receiving diuretic therapy may have symptoms of magnesium deficiency. On the other hand, administration of antacids and cathartics containing magnesium to patients with renal failure may result in hypermagnesia, a condition with severe toxic effects. Magnesium deficiency also leads to some reduction in blood and tissue thiamin levels and to a marked reduction in transketolase activity. This enzyme has been shown to reflect thiamin adequacy.

FUNCTION

In its common dietary forms, this mineral is readily absorbed from the small intestine; this process is favoured by an acid medium. Magnesium balance in the body is controlled to a great extent by the kidneys, whose tubules normally reabsorb the mineral as needed. Magnesium is an essential element in human metabolism; it functions in the work of muscles and nerves, in synthesis of proteins, and in many specific reactions such as glucose utilization, methyl group transfer and oxidative phosphorylation. This mineral acts in both soft tissues and bones as an activator for many enzymes, particularly for those concerned with the transfer of phosphate from ATP to a phosphate receptor or from a phosphorylated compound to ADP. There is evidence that magnesium is involved in themoregulation. Magnesium may have a part in treatment of atherosclerosis. Lipid deposits in the vertical valves and aortas of rats were prevented by addition of high magnesium. It was found that animals fed moderately low amounts of magnesium often developed calcified lesions in soft tissues. When these animals were fed cholesterol they were more susceptible to atherogenesis. Men who are more susceptible to cardiovascular diseases are also more likely than women to have negative magnesium balances. It has been suggested that one of magnesium's functions is to prevent accumulation of cholesterol in the blood.

Magnesium has been shown to activate many enzymes *in vitro*, particularly those concerned with transphosphorylating reactions. However, few disturbances in enzymic activity have been unequivocally established during magnesium deficiency *in vivo*. Magnesium also appears to be involved in the structure of ribosomes and nucleic acids and although it is recognized that appreciable amounts of the element occur in all fractions of the cell, very little evidence is available about the chemical states in which it exists. Changes in either the total concentration or the chemical state of magnesium within different compartments of the cell could exert a profound effect on the regulations of metabolism and the function of magnesium at the cellular level merits much further investigation.

A major problem in magnesium metabolism concerns the mechanism of its transport across biological membranes. The intracellular concentration of magnesium is more than ten times higher than that outside the cell and is maintained even when the extracellular concentration falls very low. This implies that some active process takes place, but little or no evidence for such a process has yet been found.

APPENDIX

Table - 1

Elements in Human Diet (mg/day)

Trace Element	Normal	Toxic	Lethal
Aluminium	2-45	5000	-
Arsenic	0.04-1.4	5-50	50-300
Cobalt	0.0005-1.8	500	-
Copper	0.5-6	20	175-250
Chlorine	0.5-3	20	2000
Iodine	0.1-0.2	2	35000-350,000
Iron	6-40	200	7000-35,000
Magnesium	250-380	-	-
Manganese	0.4 -10	-	-
Nickel	0.3-0.5	-	-
Selenium	0.0006-0.2	5	-
Zinc	5-40	150-600	6000

Table-2
Important Functions

Element	Function
Magnesium	Muscle tone, chlorophyll component, activates enzymes which utilise ATP.
Manganese	Enzyme activator like DNA & RNA polymerases, guanylate cyclase, metalloenzymes like pyruvate kinase, pyruvate carboxylase, arginase, hyperoxide dismutases etc.
Iron	Haemoproteins (myoglobin, haemoglobin, cytochromes) hemerythrin (oxygen transport protein in seashore worms) enzymes like acotinase, catalase, peroxidase etc, ferritin.
Cobalt	Vitamin B_{12} and B_{12} coenzymes.
Nickel	Integral component of enzymes urease, also may be involved in the action of hydrogenase.
Copper	Oxidase enzymes like tyrosinase, amino oxidase, cytochrome oxidase, ascorbate oxidase etc, haemocyanin (oxygen transport protein in insects), hydrolytic enzyme unease, ceruloplasmin (a storage protein).
Zinc	Enzymes of main metabolic pathways, synthesis of RNA, DNA and proteins like yeast aldolase, hydrolytic enzymes carbonic anhydrase, carboxy-peptidase, alkaline phosphatase dehydrogenase enzymes like aldol dehydrogenase, glutamic dehydrogenase, lactic dehydrogenase etc. Acts as

(Contd.)

Element	Function
	deaminase, enolase etc. Constuent of hormone insulin and snake venom. High concentration of zinc is found in the prostate gland and choroid of the eye and in pollen seed of plants, essential for growth and cell replication.
Selenium	Glycine reductase and glutathione peroxidase
Fluorine	Teeth and bone development

Table - 3

Effects of Some Trace Elements of the Body

Element	Deficiency	Excess
Flourine	Poor bones and teeth	Mottled teeth, bone sclerosis
Iodine	Hypothyroidism, goitre	Hyperthyroidism
Magnesium	Delirium and neuromuscular manifestations such as convulsions, tingling, twitchings, numbness and tremors, hypocalcemia	Anaesthesia, nausea, affects respiratory and Nervous systems, cardiovascular systems
Manganese	Skeletal deformities due to impaired bone growth, reduced reproductive function and depressed cholesterol synthesis, reddening of hair.	Serious and irreversible damage to the CNS and brain (ataxia)
Iron	Anemia	Hemochromatosis, lesions in gastrointestinal tract, shock and liver damage

(Contd.)

Element	Deficiency	Excess
Cobalt	Anemia and stunted growth.	Coronary failure, thyroid disfunction due to impaired accumulation of iodine.
Nickel	Dermatitics, liver changes.	Gastrointenstinal discomfort, degeneration of heart and tissue sweating leaches.
Copper	Anemia, poor bones and connective tissues, loss of hair, pig-mentation.	Stomach, irritation and nausea, reduced growth, liver damage and damage to kidney and brain, (Jaundice and Wilson's disease.
Zinc	Skin disorder, growth retardation (dwarfism), retarded sexual develop-ment and sex function in man (low fertility) affects lactation in woman, mental disorder, (aporexia nervosa).	Gastrointestinal disturbances and nausea, anemia, hinder bone development, pulmonary distress, fevers.
Selenium	Infertility, liver necrosis muscular dystrophy, leucocytes inefficient.	Cancer, deformed nails and hair.
Aluminium	not known	Deformaties in bone, osteoprosis, dysfunction of liver kidney, lungs, neuronal degeneration, Alzhemier's disease.
Arsenic	not known	Haemolysis, tetragen, anemia, skin pigmentation.

Table - 4

Estimated and Adequate Daily Intakes of Selected Trace Elements

	Trace Elements									
Age (years)	Iron (mg)	Zinc (mg)	Iodine (mg)	Copper (mg)	Manganese (mg)	Fluoride (mg)	Chromium (mg)	Selenium (mg)	Molybdenum (mg)	Magnesuim (mg)
INFANTS										
0-0.5	10	3	40	0.5-0.7	0.5-0.7	0.1-0.5	0.01-0.04	0.01-0.04	0.05-0.06	50
0.5-1	15	5	50	0.7-1.0	0.7-1.0	0.2-1.0	0.02-0.06	0.02-0.06	0.07-0.08	70
CHILDREN AND ADOLESCENTS										
1-3	15	10	70	1.0-1.5	1.0-1.5	0.5-1.5	0.02-0.08	0.02-0.08	0.05-0.1	150
4-6	10	10	90	1.5-2.0	1.5-2.0	1.0-2.5	0.03-0.12	0.03-0.12	0.06-0.15	200
7-10	10	10	120	2.0-2.5	2.0-3.0	1.5-2.5	0.05-0.2	0.05-0.2	0.10-0.3	250
11+	10	15	150	2.0-3.0	2.5-5.0	1.5-2.5	0.05-0.2	0.05-0.2	0.15-0.5	350
ADULTS										
	10	15	150	2.0-3.0	2.5-5.0	1.5-4.0	0.05-0.2	0.05-0.2	0.15-0.5	350

From Recommended Dietary Allowances, Revised 1979. Food and Nutrition Board. National Academy of Sciences—National Research Council, Washington, D.C.

FURTHER READINGS

1. "Biological Aspects of Metals and Metal-related Diseases." Edited by Bibubhandra Sarkar, Raven Press, New York, 1983.
2. "Nutrition." Chaney and Ross M., Surjeet Publications, Delhi, 1979.
3. "Some Aspects on the Role of Metal Ions in Biological Systems." D. Banerjee, *Everyman's Science*, 30, 176, 1994.
4. "Nutrition throughout the Life Cycle." S.R. Williams and B.S. Worthington-Roberts, Times/Mosby College Publishing, St. Louis, 1988.
5. "Food and Nutrition Research." Report of the ARC/MRC Committee, Elsevier Publication Company, Amsterdam 1974.
6. "Introduction to Nutrition." Henrietta Flack, Macmillan Publishing Company, New York 1981.
7. "Modern Nutrition in Health and Disease." Goodhart Robert S. and Maurice E. Shils, Philadelphia, Lea & Febiger, 1980.

Dr. Amit Krishna De M.Sc. Ph.D. FNESA, FAEB, FICN is the Assistant Executive Secretary of the Indian Science Congress Association, Calcutta. He is also involved in active teaching in Acharya Jagadish Chandra College and Department of Biochemistry, Calcutta University as Invited Lecturer.

He has won the 1991 Sm. Kamal Satbir Award (Young Scientist) from Indian Council of Medical Research (ICMR), New Delhi and Dr. S.R. Dasgupta Memorial Award from Indian Pharmacological Society (IPS), Calcutta, in 1992.

He is Fellow of National Environmental Science Academy, Academy of Environmental Biology and International College of Nutrition .